Never stop unlearning

The author is donating 100% of book proceeds to mental health charities.

"Kunal Gupta's bold journey is a masterclass in intentional living. *UNLEARNING* is an example of crafting a life that's uniquely yours, encouraging us **not to be afraid of living life on our own terms.**"

"Reading *UNLEARNING* feels like engaging in **a heart-to-heart with a wise friend**. Kunal's insights are as profound as they are practical."

"From the boardrooms of New York to the streets of Lisbon, Kunal reminds us of the power of self-discovery. *UNLEARNING* acts as **a compass for those daring enough** to venture off the beaten path."

"*UNLEARNING* serves both as a memoir and a philosophical guidebook for the modern soul. **His unconventional choices and raw experiences offer a breath of fresh air** in a world of conformity."

"I've faced many of the personal challenges Kunal describes. *UNLEARNING* **feels like a trusted friend**, helping you navigate the turbulent waters of modern life and business."

"*UNLEARNING* addresses the existential questions of our generation with both grace and grit. It's **a must-read for anyone feeling lost in the digital age.**"

"His bold experiences, from daily meditation to moving to Portugal on a whim, stand as an inspiring example of the power of curiosity and courage. Kunal's **stories are as inspiring as they are relatable**."

"*UNLEARNING* offers a refreshing perspective on life. His journey is a reminder that **life isn't about fitting in**, but about discovering ourselves. It's a must-read for those seeking a life beyond the ordinary."

UNLEARNING

IS EXPERIMENTS THAT TRANSFORMED MY LIFE

KUNAL GUPTA

SPARK

CONTENTS

I have no right to call myself one who knows. I was one who seeks, and I still am, but I no longer seek in the stars or in the books; I'm beginning to hear the teachings of my blood pulsing within me. My story isn't pleasant, it's not sweet and harmonious like the invented stories; it tastes of folly and bewilderment, of madness and dream, like the life of all people who no longer want to lie to themselves.

-Herman Hesse

INTRODUCTION

FIFTEEN EXPERIMENTS THAT TRANSFORMED MY LIFE

Step by step, let whatever happens happen. Real change will come when it is brought about, not by your ego, but by reality. Awareness releases reality to change you.

-Anthony De Mello

When I woke up that morning, I had no idea everything was about to change forever.

I was living in Toronto at the time. The day started with my usual routine: walk to the office, which was down the street; log in; answer a few emails. Between meetings, emails, text messages, and social interactions, there wasn't much else in my daily life.

It was barely 9 a.m., but the bright sun was spilling in through the big windows of the office. As the sunlight turned my computer screen into a glorified mirror, I found myself in a staring contest with my own reflection. The rest of my team had yet to show up, and in the quiet office that morning, I noticed something different inside me.

I felt bored.

Boredom was a new feeling.

Seven years into my business, which I started right out of school, working long hours and long days were the norm. There was always something broken to fix.

Now, sitting there with this unfamiliar boredom, I went through a familiar mental checklist.

Over the years, I have learned there are four problems that can arise in any business:

1. a product or service issue;

2. a client, competition, or market issue;

3. a people, process, or talent issue;

4. a cash or funding issue

If two of these issues are present, it's stressful; three, the business outlook is not great; and four, there is no business, and people are fooling themselves.

Until that moment, there had always been only one or two things broken in my business—rarely three and never all four. It was always a game of spinning plates: constantly fixing one, thinking everything would be good once it was solved, but then having to solve the next, and the next, and so on.

It was as exhilarating as it was exhausting, never allowing myself to feel satisfied.

Fast forward seven years of plate spinning and, for the first time ever, nothing was broken. Nothing needed fixing.

The mental checklist:

Product? It was working as expected, for once.

Clients? Really happy: nobody had left in over a year.

Team? The team was focused, productive, and seemed satisfied.

Cash? The business was approaching profitability, revenue was growing nicely, and we had lots of money in the bank.

Wow, I thought. We did it. The business is finally running as expected. I can finally feel satisfied.

The feeling of boredom still present, my mind naturally shifted toward my personal life. Another mental checklist.

Love? I was in a serious, committed relationship; we were living together. All good.

Family? My sister lived a ten-minute walk away; my parents a twenty-minute drive. I saw them frequently, and we enjoyed spending time together.

Health? I was eating well. I had a personal trainer and was working out a few times a week. I felt strong and healthy.

Friends? I was going out, drinking with friends every week, and hosting parties every month. I was surrounded by a lot of energy and fun. I'd just come back from a European trip with my closest friends and genuinely felt connected to others.

Clothes? I was traveling to London for business often, where I found an undiscovered British clothing brand that fit my figure well and filled my closet.

Home? My beautiful apartment was on the fifty-fourth floor of the Shangri-La, a luxury condominium and hotel in downtown Toronto. I had a view overlooking the entire city and a valet who would park my car and take my groceries up to my suite. Looking back, I'm grateful for the privilege I unknowingly had (and still do).

As I completed my life audit, confusion started to set in.

In my business life, everything was exactly as I wanted.

In my personal life, I had it all.

Thanks to a lot of hard work, tremendous support from others, and a bit of luck, the things that felt important at that moment in my life were the things I had.

"I made it", I said to myself, quietly sitting in my office. I had reached the top of the mountain I'd been climbing. After years of running, I had finished the race.

By then it was a few minutes past nine. My buzzing mind quickly quieted.

"I made it", I said again, hoping to feel something.

A longer pause followed.

I didn't feel anything.

Then an unexpected thought arose: "It" isn't here.

I expected to feel satisfied. I expected to feel successful. I expected to feel happy. Yet I felt none of these.

I had been climbing the mountain of achievement with the assumption that some combination of satisfaction, success, and happiness would be waiting at the top for me. I reached the summit, looked around . . . and the feelings I was expecting were nowhere to be found.

That was the moment everything changed.

In that moment I began to turn inward.

In that moment I began to challenge the values and beliefs that had led me to the top of the achievement mountain.

In that moment I hit the reset button on my life. And begun my journey in learning how to live.

Through childhood into adulthood, I lived like a sponge, blindly soaking up the values and belief systems of my parents, culture, teachers, and society.

My journey of learning how to live involved wringing out

the sponge in order to begin the process of choosing my own values and beliefs. **Unaware of what I actually believed to be true anymore, I had only one choice: to experiment.**

An experiment, by definition, means not knowing the outcome I am going to get. I may have a theory or idea about possible outcomes, but the definitive or expected outcome is unknown. An experiment with an expected outcome is a plan, not an experiment.

Looking back, I can see clearly what was impossible to see then: a new journey had started. Everyone close to me began to notice changes in me—changes I wasn't always aware of, as they were happening deep inside.

I had begun to challenge life by choosing to experiment with it.

In the years to come, I would design and implement a series of experiments that changed everything in my life. This book is a collection of some of these experiments and how they've shaped me.

The purpose of this book is not to tell others how to live. It is to share how I have learned how to live.

My hope is that the reader finds inspiration to experiment with life in their own unique way, and discovers how to live in a way that's uniquely theirs.

This book is my journey of **unlearning**.

EXPERIMENT REFLECTIONS

Boredom can be a positive catalyst for change. Recognizing dissatisfaction can spark the journey towards a more fulfilling life.

Spinning plates in business or life is not sustainable, it is essential to find satisfaction beyond continuous problem-solving and fire fighting.

Awakening can happen when one turns inwards and challenges inherited values and beliefs, to start to choose new ones that are more aligned.

UNLEARNING

CONSUMERISM

TWO YEARS WITHOUT BUYING ANY STUFF

To be without some of the things you want is an indispensable part of happiness.

-Bertrand Russell

I used to believe that buying stuff would bring me happiness. I must have wanted to be really happy, because I bought a lot of stuff. That habit might have gone on forever were it not for a romantic crush.

At the time I was traveling frequently to London. On one trip, a woman at a conference caught my eye. We immediately hit it off. We didn't talk about business, despite the context. She asked me out for a drink in Covent Garden, a popular tourist area in central London. She was "proper" British, and very much on time. I was late, a habit I've now accepted. I must have been cute enough for her to tolerate my tardiness, at least for a while.

I found myself attracted to her, especially the way she dressed.

She introduced me to Reiss, a British clothing brand that had been popularized by Kate Middleton during her engagement to Prince William. Reiss was undiscovered and unavailable in North America, which only added to the allure for me. Feeling courageous, I asked, "Hey, can we go shopping at Reiss together sometime?"

On my next visit to London a few weeks later, we did exactly that.

To be honest, it was intimidating to go shopping with a

woman I had a crush on. It was like taking a woman out to a fancy restaurant just to impress her. In this case, she did not get an expensive meal—but I got new clothes.

No surprise, I walked out of the shopping mall that day with both hands full of Reiss bags.

The pattern was set. Every few months during my visit to London, I made a pilgrimage to Reiss. I even convinced one of the store managers to give me a 25 percent discount under the table. As a visitor, I learned about the sales tax refund trick that saved me another 23 percent. The fact that I now got almost 50 percent off everything was enabling; it gave me permission in my mind to buy anything.

I regularly overspent, exceeding my income and I found every justification to assure myself it was acceptable.

It is often said that humans are logical beings who sometimes experience emotions. However, I have come to understand that **humans are emotional beings who sometimes use logic to justify emotions.**

My crush on the British woman eventually fizzled. It turns out that connecting over a fashion brand was not a great indicator of long-term potential. Although my interest in her faded, my interest in Reiss did not. It only grew.

A few years later, something unexpected happened.

After returning from another business trip and Reiss-shopathon, I unpacked my carry-on suitcase and hung my clothes back in my perfectly organized walk-in closet, where all my attire was arranged by color. As I hung up yet another new Reiss dress shirt—I realized I was hanging it next to an identical Reiss dress shirt. Same color, same cut, same size. My shirt now had a twin.

I had bought the exact same clothes I already owned. And not on purpose. It would be one thing to do it intentionally, but this was completely accidental.

I've often been curious about what in life comes from intention. Many positive and welcome developments may be accidental, whereas negative and unwelcome developments may be intentional. The underlying reason something happened, or did not happen, is important.

I'd bought the same clothes with the same label from the same store in the same size, due to a total lack of awareness.

An alarm bell went off inside me. My addiction to shopping had gone too far. That day, the seed was planted in my mind that my attitude toward owning stuff had to change. But I had no idea what was about to happen.

A few weeks later, a close friend got married in San Francisco. Indian weddings are another great example of consumerism gone too far. If the Reiss accident planted the seed, being immersed in an Indian wedding watered it.

On the Air Canada flight home to Toronto, a film on the in-flight entertainment system caught my attention: *The Lightbulb Conspiracy.*

The documentary shows how the past century of consumerism has become part of the fabric of our society. In 1920, the chairman of a German lightbulb company signed a pact with all the lightbulb manufacturers in Germany to reduce the capacity of their products. Why? Because the faster bulbs burn out, the more frequently they need to be replaced. Back then, the average bulb lasted 2,500 hours. Today it only lasts 1,000 hours, despite a century of science and innovation.

There are other examples of executives featured in the documentary who deliberately created a system to force people to buy more stuff. One CEO of General Motors reshaped the automotive industry in the 1950s so that a new car would be released every year instead of every eight to ten.

And Steve Jobs invented a specialized screw for Apple products so that customers could not change batteries easily, forcing them to buy a whole new product.

As the documentary progressed, anger rose inside me. People were being tricked by design.

Curious to explore my own privilege of being able to buy anything I wanted on a whim, I came up with an experiment—the first of many to be shared in this book.

For six months, I would not buy anything material. That meant no clothes, no books, no furniture, no gifts. My purchases would be limited to food and other necessities, transportation, accommodation, and experiences: yoga classes, going to the movies, digital subscriptions, and the like.

No one knew about my experiment. Choosing not to tell anyone gave me privacy—and less fear of failure. Truthfully, in my heart of hearts, I didn't think I could actually do it.

For years I'd lived on one extreme of the consumption spectrum; now the experiment was to hang out at the other extreme. For me, this felt very challenging at the time. But I was committed to resetting my relationship with stuff—and not just because of the Reiss accident. Deep down, I was starting to challenge a long-held belief that buying stuff would bring me happiness.

It took my sister all of three weeks to catch on with my

experiment. I have one sibling, which has proven to be more than enough, since we're very close. We are one year and one day apart in age; she was the best birthday gift I've ever received. Despite being the younger sibling, she behaves as if she's older. Of course, when it's convenient, she can play the role of younger sister remarkably well.

She had grown accustomed to me buying her chocolates, handicrafts, and random airport souvenirs on every trip I went on, because my addiction was not restricted to buying only for me. Whether a trip was for business or fun, I would often return with gifts for her.

My sister is smart. She noticed I was still traveling but that the gifts had stopped. Like a lawyer questioning a witness on the stand, she began her inquisition one day about what was wrong with me.

I caved and explained my experiment.

She listened carefully and attentively, then asked more challenging questions. My resolve still did not weaken. When that didn't work, she reverted to younger sister mode and began to protest. Once she realized she wasn't going to be successful, she expressed her frustration—and then moved on to other matters.

My experiment had survived its first challenge. My trial

commitment to anti-consumerism was in full swing now. As a result, many subtle changes began to surface in my everyday life.

Take, for example, yoga. My yoga practice was relatively new, and my yoga mat, which was a hand me down, had a small rip in one corner. For months, every single time I did downward dog or plank pose, I would notice the small rip and make a mental note to buy a new mat. But then I would forget to do so.

Once the experiment started, I stopped making the mental note to replace the mat. The distraction disappeared as I started to accept reality as it was.

Winter in Canada is not for the faint of heart. Canadians have heaps of sweaters to survive comfortably. When I get excited about something, I move my arms a lot, which leads to holes forming in the armpit area of my sweaters. Previously, my habitual pattern was to throw out the sweater and buy a new one. In the midst of this experiment, that was no longer an option. For the first time, I started to sew up the holes myself.

Repairing old sweaters was not only good for the wider environment but also my internal environment. Mending became a highly meditative experience that, to my surprise, I looked forward to. It sparked a sense of satisfaction and provided a hit of dopamine—the "feel good" hormone in the brain's pleasure center—that comes from having accomplished something or buying something. To use my hands to do something other than typing away at a computer all day was a novelty.

I had loved my new Reiss clothes, but with my old sweaters, the intention was different. With the Reiss wardrobe, it was all about appearance and the external perception of value. But by fixing my old sweaters, I treated clothes with greater respect.

I stopped buying stuff for myself—and for others. This part of my experiment was uncomfortable. I had to overcome my fear of being potentially judged for not showing up to someone's place with a gift.

On the other hand, it saved me so much time. I love a good efficiency hack. But the biggest surprise was the mental space it unlocked for me. The freedom. The release. There was no need to make choices. The choice was simple: it was always no.

Constraints can be liberating.

Being vegetarian has taught me that. In the past, I was always the first to order at restaurants, since usually there were only a few possible options. Now that not eating meat and animal products has become more widespread, there are vegan and vegetarian restaurants. I find it confusing, not liberating, to order at these places, since everything is an option. My solution to this problem is often to ask the waiter to decide and to surprise me. Decision paralysis: solved.

Six months into my anti-consumerism experiment, I was absolutely loving it.

Especially the fact that I was still undercover; my sister was the only person who knew. One morning while meditating, I realized that although I hit the six-month mark, the experiment was still quite juicy for me and I had more to learn. I wanted to continue.

The experiment continued for two years. Two years without buying a single material item. When it finally ended, it was not because I had a list of things I was desperate to purchase. Rather, it was because minimalism had become a part of me—my identity, my personality, my values, my beliefs.

I understood that less can, in fact, be more. Buying stuff does not bring me happiness.

The knowledge that less can be more and stuff doesn't equal happiness is not that big a surprise. But knowledge alone is not enough. Knowledge is a commodity: we can treasure it, horde it, value it— without ever choosing to act on it.

Experience, on the other hand, is unique. **Experience is valuable. And knowledge mixed with experience is how wisdom is born.** Wisdom is what my experiment gave me.

The experiment was no longer juicy for me—its purpose was complete. Just like I had outgrown my crush on the British woman, I'd also outgrown my reliance on buying stuff. The former took a few months; the latter a few years.

Years later, despite the advertisements that tell me otherwise, I understand that buying stuff does not bring me happiness. I can now take a spontaneous trip without packing anything. It's not only *possible* to go from here to there with no dependence on stuff, it's *freeing*. My relationship with stuff has changed forever.

One of my favorite books of all time is Mitch Albom's *Tuesdays with Morrie*. I'll never forget the moment Morrie says, "The culture we have does not make people feel good about themselves. And you have to be strong enough to say if the culture doesn't work, don't buy it."

My experiment was inspired by reaching the top of the

achievement mountain, an ambition that was influenced heavily by the culture I grew up in. But at the top, all I felt was dissatisfaction—not the feeling I'd expected. The culture didn't work for me.

Sure, I chose not to buy stuff, but more than that: I chose to not buy the culture. This choice was me opening a door deeper within and having the courage to walk through it.

And that is how I unlearned consumerism.

EXPERIMENT REFLECTIONS

Happiness cannot be bought; it comes from within. The culture of more often left me feeling empty and dissatisfied after the temporary high wore off.

Letting go of material possessions taught me that contentment is found in experiences and relationships, not things.

The most significant shift was choosing not to buy into a culture that doesn't align with my values. This choice opened a door to deeper self-discovery and freedom.

UNLEARNING

COMFORT

ONE HUNDRED NIGHTS SLEEPING ON PEOPLE'S COUCHES

I have learned that from water, from the river, and from the eyes of every child I have met, that I can learn everything; that there is no teacher anywhere except the whole world.

-Herman Hesse

A fter two years of not buying things, I began to be curious about what the next experiment would be. The first experiment had helped me reset my relationship with stuff. Now I wanted to reset my relationship with my physical space.

Once again, the catalyst happened to be a documentary: this time a series called *The Kindness Diaries*.

The film followed Leon, an Australian man, who was trying to test a thesis that the world is, in fact, kind. This man decided, with no money and no belongings except the clothes on his back, that he was going to travel around the entire world, relying solely on the kindness of others.

First spoiler alert: he did it.

Second spoiler alert: the world is, in fact, kind. The kindness Leon experienced in each episode often brought me to tears. I found the story fascinating. It was the right inspiration, at the right time for me.

The question came as I sat quietly on my sister's couch, watching the show: What's my version of this?

The experiment to experience the kindness of others had been done before. I had no doubt people would offer me food and stay from a place of kindness, but I didn't believe I would learn enough.

I had challenged a belief that buying stuff would bring me happiness. My experiment had proven this was not the case.

Now I wanted to challenge a belief that my physical space is responsible for my happiness. *This* piqued my curiosity. It felt juicy.

I decided to challenge myself by going "houseless" for half a year as my next experiment with life.

The use of the term *houseless* instead of *homeless* is intentional. For me it was a choice, and I recognize that, for many people who are actually unhoused, underhoused, or experiencing homelessness, it is not a choice.

By that point, I had already given up my fancy apartment on the fifty-fourth floor at the Shangri-La. I was living in the second bedroom of my sister's apartment in downtown Toronto with very few belongings, and traveling every week for business. For this experiment, however, houseless meant staying in a physical space where I did not have influence or control over it.

The spaces I could control were my sister's apartment, my parents' house, and the many hotels and Airbnbs I stayed in around the world while traveling. All of these were some version of home for me.

But "going houseless" meant staying in spaces other than these for half a year. This was to be the wildest experiment I could design. I had no idea just how much I was about to learn.

It was the first week of January, in the peak cold of winter in Toronto. My friend Alex lived five minutes down the street from my sister. I called him bright and early one Monday morning.

"Hey Alex," I said. "Happy New Year. Can I stay at your place tonight?"

Long pause.

"Everything okay?" he asked, wondering what had gotten into me.

"Yep, everything's great," I said, sidestepping the question beneath the question. He graciously said yes, I think from a place of curiosity. After all, it was not the first time a friend had quietly wondered: What's Kunal up to this time?

I had known Alex for ten years. Asking him felt like a safe starting point for my experiment. What few belongings I had left were at my sister's, and just a few minutes away was a friendly and familiar face.

Alex had recently gotten engaged, and I had not yet spent any quality time with his fiancée, Nina. I crashed at their place for two nights on a sofa bed in their home office. The space was so compact. It was the ultimate game of Tetris living.

They cooked vegetarian food for me, I taught them how to meditate, and we shared deep conversations late into the night.

Nina opened up to me, and I got to know her in a way that would have been difficult in the usual group settings. Most of all, I really enjoyed seeing the two of them together and admired how they interacted. All of this from simply sleeping at their place for a few nights, while we were all working in our respective offices and businesses during the day.

As part of the experiment, I decided not to tell Alex and Nina why I asked to stay at their place. They were open enough to just go with it. They trusted I had my reasons, both for doing it and for not sharing why.

I also decided not to bring them a gift. After two years without buying any stuff, I didn't want to backtrack. I also didn't cook for them or offer any acts of service out of the ordinary. I didn't want this to feel like a transaction for any of us.

Too often, how people connect in the modern world can feel transactional, even for people who are well-educated, earning respectable incomes, and generally financially independent.

For example, the simple gesture of paying for someone's meal is often accepted with a grin and "the next one is on me." I wonder if this is to make the receiver feel better about receiving. When I pay for a restaurant bill, it sometimes feels like the impact of my gift is diminished when the receiver makes me feel like there is a scorecard that needs to be balanced.

Avoiding the temptation of bringing something or doing something for my hosts forced me to learn how to receive. It felt uncomfortable.

As this new experiment launched, I was a minimalist traveling with nothing but a backpack: a wanderer through life, looking only for a place to stay and something to eat.

I found my first attempt of this new experiment with Alex and Nina interesting—and I wanted more. Later during that first week of January, I called my friend Adrian, who lived outside the city.

"Hey Adrian," I said. "Can I come stay with you this weekend?"

"Everything okay?" he asked, in a confused tone echoing Alex's.

"Yep, everything's great."

Asking Adrian was more difficult than asking Alex. Although the conversation was similar, I noticed a nervousness inside me. My friendship with Alex had held steady for over a decade, whereas Adrian and I had only connected in the past year. But we had developed a strong enough bond, mostly through meditation, that I felt safe enough to ask.

I was starting to collect my learnings.

The act of asking turned out to be more difficult—and less common—than I realized. The unconscious script was firmly established, especially in the era of online commerce: be independent, solve your own problems, and don't bother other people, they are busy. There were very few instances on a daily basis when I asked someone else for help. Knowing that I would not be bringing any gift made it that much more uncomfortable to ask. Learning to ask required overcoming those nerves. Home, I realized, had always been a solo activity; now it involved teamwork.

With no car at the time, I took the train an hour outside the city to where Adrian lived with his wife. He picked me up from the station on that cold and snowy winter day. As we pulled into the driveway of his home in the countryside, he said, "Oh, by the way, I have two dogs."

Fear seized me. At that point, I had never lived with dogs. This is what I love, and love to hate, about experiments: I cannot control the circumstances.

Adrian had two large huskies, the classic Canadian dog. He told me not to worry if they got overexcited, and said, "Even if it looks like they're going to bite you, they won't actually do it."

My fear of possibly being eaten by two large dogs was growing by the second. Noticing my fear, I turned to my meditation practice. I began controlling my breath. I coached myself to stay calm and kept my mind focused on my healthy body . . . rather than worrying about my soon-to-be-bitten body.

We walked into his home, and the huskies were silent. They came up, sniffed me, and walked away. Adrian turned to me and said, "I've never seen them act like that when meeting someone new."

I was saved, thanks to meditation. It is well-known that dogs can sense fear. It follows, then, that they can also sense calm. I chose to feed them some calm, not my limbs.

We all had a beautiful weekend together. I'd never met Adrian's wife, Pam, who was a doctor. I meditated with Pam and learned more about her life. The three of us cooked together, went for hikes, enjoyed late-night hot tub sessions, and spent the weekend connecting on so many different levels. I even played with their dogs—an unexpected development for me. Living with two giant huskies is not something I would have ever chosen to do on my own. If he'd told me about them beforehand, I probably would have shied away from asking for a place to stay.

The lessons from this experiment continued to pile up. I had discovered that **not knowing can sometimes be better than knowing.**

As I stepped into people's homes, telling them nothing about what I was doing and why, I noticed that no one needed anything. The privilege of extra space and stuff was everywhere in plain sight for me to see, at least amongst my connections.

But as I would come to learn across many experiments, **signs of discomfort are more often than not correlated with growth.**

I like to pull at the threads, despite the discomfort, sensing intuitively that they have the potential to lead somewhere special. I first had to learn how to ask; now I was learning how to receive, without relying on the comfortable crutch of giving in the same breath as receiving.

After a few successful attempts of going houseless under my belt, my confidence with this experiment grew. I began to take more risks.

In the cities I most frequented—Toronto, New York, and London—I continued to stay with friends. Then friends of friends. And eventually, complete strangers.

One memorable experience was a weekend in Lisbon. I would try couchsurfing. I was replacing a five-star hotel with a five-cushion adventure that I could only assume would have a side of awkward morning conversations after sharing a space with a complete stranger.

The first night, I stayed with a young journalist from Estonia who had only recently moved to Portugal. She was a young, strong, confident Eastern European; she showed me Lisbon—including a lookout point near where I live now. As she shared her life journey with me, I appreciated her trust, as well as the time and effort she spent to make me feel at home.

The second night, I stayed with a Portuguese pilot who was close to my age. The next morning, he took me to his flying club and offered to take me up in his tiny plane.

I'd been on a lot of planes in my life, but nothing that small and fragile. It felt like the wind was doing more work than the engine. At one point, while we were flying over Lisbon, he let me fly. Then, when I wasn't paying attention, he cut the engine—and the plane began to nosedive. It turned out he was secretly videotaping the practical joke on his phone, hoping for a reaction.

Sadly, he was disappointed. Just like with Adrian's huskies, I had switched on my meditation calmness and stayed completely calm.

Couchsurfing as a man is clearly different than as a woman, and as I reflected on the weekend of couchsurfing my way through Lisbon, I realized that I probably would not have done this if I was a woman. Another reminder of the privilege I enjoy.

Throughout this experiment, I was still CEO of my technology business, which at the time had four global offices, hundreds of clients and millions in revenue. With a meeting-filled Chief Everything Officer daily schedule, I would sleep on someone's couch almost every night—and didn't tell anyone in my world. Nobody knew: not my parents, not my friends, not my team, not my investors. Whenever my clients asked where I was staying, I'd tell a white lie and say a hotel or Airbnb.

Keeping the experiment private was important to me. **Often when things are shared, they become tainted with the fears and insecurities others project onto them.** I knew people would challenge and criticize my approach to experimenting with what home is. I did not want their judgment to get in the way of my growth.

Anthony De Mello, who passed away the year I was born, wrote: "What others think of you often says more about them than it does about you." This teaching has given me the courage to be less concerned about what others think of my choices and more curious about what I can learn.

Nevertheless, I did break down twice.

Three months into the experiment, I was walking alone on Third Avenue in New York on a crisp March evening after dinner. All of a sudden, I started to cry uncontrollably on the street. I had stayed with six different people in seven days. My body and brain were exhausted from my daytime schedule. I was tired from not sleeping comfortably and annoyed from the lack of any personal space. I had hit my edge and felt lost without the feeling of home.

After the emotional release, which was necessary, I reminded myself that this is why I was doing the experiment. An experiment has no known results. It is not all going to be rainbows and sunshine. I had chosen to go houseless to see where my edge was. Now that I had reached it, I found growth—and felt a hunger for more of it.

The second time I broke was in September, in London, staying in a place where I didn't feel safe. There were a lot of random people in the house, so I locked myself in the bedroom, where I started to cry. And continued to cry. The tears came from a place of discomfort with the discomfort.

That night, I wrote in my journal. Many of the words in this chapter were taken from that journal entry. I journaled about how grateful I was to all of the people who had opened their homes to me, and the insights this experiment had provided. Paging back through my journal, I saw the list of lessons I had collected over the nights I had been houseless and a thought crystallized: There's nothing more I need to learn right now. I feel satisfied.

That is when I concluded the experiment, a few months early before the end of the year.

One hundred seven nights with thirty-two different people in nine countries. Not the six months I had originally envisioned—but the experiment felt complete. I no longer needed to prove anything, not to myself or anyone else.

This was one juicy experiment, packed with life lessons on

how to live. I experienced kindness, which was the original spark.

I learned that **home is not something on the outside, but something on the inside.** After being pushed to my edge, I had no choice but to turn inward for the feeling of home that was not available to me on the outside.

After the draining routine of working twelve hours a day, flying each week to some city or another, then staying in a space I wasn't in control of, I learned how to further cultivate my mental state. When there was only discomfort around me, I learned to find comfort within.

I learned that when people open up their home, they open up their life. I found a new level of intimacy and vulnerability that was lacking in most social settings. I discovered more about some people in twenty-four hours of being in their space than from a decade of friendship. And I also observed how home was something on the inside for them, too; they were not overly attached to their space or stuff.

I got to witness how people live. I stayed with people who had pets of all types, as well as young kids and babies or sick relatives. I stayed with people who could not afford a lot, and with others who could. I stayed with some people in partnerships who were constantly in disagreement, and some who were constantly inspired by one another. They all taught me so much by allowing me to witness how they lived.

After going houseless for one hundred and seven nights, I hit the reset button on my relationship with space in a way I needed at that moment in my life. The experiment taught me how to ask, how to receive, how to connect, how to empathize, and how to be more open. It helped me challenge the belief that I needed to live in a fancy apartment or home to be happy. Home was not about the physicality of the space; it was about the meaning I put into it.

And that is how I unlearned comfort.

❁

EXPERIMENT REFLECTIONS

The feeling of home is an internal state, cultivated through meaningful connections and emotional grounding, not tied to a specific location.

Going houseless challenged me to learn how to find comfort and security from within, not from my physical spaces.

Intimacy and vulnerability with others reveal that home is about the relationships I nurture, not the physical space I hangout in.

UNLEARNING
DARKNESS

TEN YEARS MEDITATING DAILY

The mind is everything; what you think, you become.

-Buddha

The trip was my girlfriend's idea, not mine. We were supposedly on vacation on an island off the coast of Mexico—but it wasn't the kind of vacation I was used to taking. My jet-setting lifestyle meant traveling to New York, London, or Dubai, not a random tiny hippie island off the coast of Mexico. For fear of getting sick, I barely ate anything and prayed every time I took a sip of water.

My girlfriend at the time had convinced me to join her for a yoga retreat which, like Mexico, was something new to me. On the first morning, when a rooster woke me abruptly from deep sleep, it didn't feel much like a "retreat." I felt out of my comfort zone physically and emotionally. I was not looking forward to the days that followed.

We rushed downstairs, late—as usual—to the 6 a.m. start. I had no idea what the schedule was and made no effort to find out. The first surprise was that the yoga retreat was in Spanish: a language I did not speak. The instructor said 'respira profundamente' which I mistakenly thought meant 'stand up'. So there I was, the only one standing in a room full of seated yogis. It took me a moment to realize why everyone was staring and then my face turned red, as I quietly sat back down.

We were all seated uncomfortably on the floor. Everyone else looked far more comfortable than I was, sitting cross legged. I adjusted my posture, trying not to disturb anyone but managing to disturb everyone.

The teacher opened with a short tale, in Spanglish, and then explained how to meditate. He first focused on instructing us on how to sit, which I found challenging, and then about focusing all of our attention on our breath or body.

The session started. It was my first time meditating. We always remember our firsts.

Eyes closed, sitting uncomfortably, a wave of peace washed over me. I noticed my breath, possibly for the first time in my life. I noticed sensations in my legs and arms. I noticed the thoughts beginning to slow down in my mind. A smile came naturally to my face.

When the gong rang, the meditation was done. What felt like a few hours turned out to be only ten minutes. Upon opening my eyes, I felt different. I was in.

This unexpected experience inspired my next experiment: to see what would happen if I truly committed to meditation. More than a decade later, I continue to meditate daily without fail.

While meditation alone has not changed my life, it has enabled *me* to change my life.

For me, meditation has been the most powerful tool to explore and build myself. It's a flashlight that helps me see in the dark, especially in the moments I feel lost. It helps me live with the lights on, revealing how many years I spent living with the lights off.

Like most of my experiments, my journey with meditation has been, in one word, intense. I have read hundreds of books, participated in countless weeklong and ten-day silent retreats, and meditated often with groups.

With this decade-plus experiment, meditation quickly became my identity. In the early years, no one could have a conversation with me *without* me bringing up meditation. I would joke that I only had two states: either in meditation, or talking about meditation. I was that guy. My sister and parents found me annoying. I got many eyerolls. No doubt, I am intense about meditation . . . and the irony of that doesn't escape me.

One afternoon while waiting for a flight in the lounge at Laguardia Airport in New York City, I sat quietly in meditation. As I came out of it, a fellow traveler next to me asked me if I was meditating. His gentle curiosity was an open door for me to share passionately the nuances of meditation. It had struck me that I was preaching tranquility with the intensity of a storm.

During my friend Alex's wedding reception, there was a lull during dinner and I gently guided the nine other guests seated at my table in a closed-eye meditation in the middle of a bustling and noisy room. It was yet another example of me bringing the practice to people who showed curiosity in unexpected places and ways. The point I was trying to make was simple though: meditation is available and accessible, at any moment I choose to access it.

Reflecting back on my experiment with meditation, I realized that in Mexico, I'd experienced "beginner's luck"—despite my positive first experience, I quickly learned that meditation was not always so inviting though. There were many challenges I faced that are uncommon and have shaped how I have built a solid foundation of meditation for over a decade now.

A few lessons I have learned over the years:

The first lesson: Let go of my desire to control thoughts and any expectations of what my thoughts should be.

My thoughts are like water flowing in a river. My desire to stop thinking about something was like placing rocks in the river to stop the flow. It was wasted effort, as the water would still find a way through. Like the water, my thoughts are always flowing. Meditation is not about trying to control the water stream; it's about learning to lift myself out of the water stream, sit on the riverbank, and watch it go by without getting caught in it.

The second lesson: I am not as unique as I might believe.

The yoga retreat in Mexico was not the first time I'd been nudged toward meditation. But when people suggested it earlier, my immediate response was always: "Meditation isn't for me. My mind is too active to be stilled." It took a while—and many moments of humility—to realize that I am not the only one who thinks. Now, when others say some version of this to me, my gentle response is, "Do you really think you're the only one with a mind overflowing with thoughts?"

The third lesson: Meditation is not about relaxation.

When I first started the meditation experiment, I expected it to help relax my mind. Just as my body feels relaxed after a massage, my mind would be relaxed after meditation. I expected it to be like taking my mind to a spa. The disappointing reality is that my mind rarely felt like it was at a spa; it was always thinking.

After five hundred days of committed meditation each morning, something shifted. Meditation became a process to strengthen my mind, the same way the gym strengthens my body. It may lead to moments of relaxation, but its purpose is to strengthen my mind, not relax it.

The fourth lesson: Diversity of technique is a good thing.

Similar to having a varied diet, savoring different foods at different times, a varied approach to meditation is helpful. Many meditation teachers preach their specific brand of meditation and shame people who are not committed enough to the particular technique day in and day out. That's the equivalent to a food brand saying I can only eat their products for every meal, every day.

I have learned, the hard way, that diversity in technique is helpful, not hurtful. No one told me that, despite the number of books, teachers, and retreats I was exposed to. Try different techniques and do not be overly attached to any one of them.

The fifth lesson: Variety of practice is a good thing.

A strong meditation practice has many layers that build on and support one another.

First is my daily practice, be it two minutes or twenty minutes. This is like taking out the kitchen trash. If I don't do it after a few days, things start to get smelly and stinky. Best I take out the trash each day.

Next is my weekly practice, which is a longer meditation,

or joining a group of people meditating. This is like tidying up my home and putting everything in its place.

And on a monthly basis, I give the home a deep scrubbing by taking a few days on retreat or simply stepping away from my day-to-day life. To do something different, possibly meditative, possibly not.

The sixth lesson: Meditation is not a solo sport.

I didn't talk about my experiment with meditation with others much during the first year. Looking back, I wish I had. I struggled with it and felt shy to talk about it, as I felt I was just a beginner.

However once I began to surround myself with like-minded people, my meditation practice grew and deepened. Having meaningful, insightful conversations and access to community became critical for me over the years. A lot of stuff comes up in meditation, and I learned that I don't have to process it all alone.

And the most important lesson: How to know if it's working.

Meditation is not about how I feel while practicing. It is called *practice*, and it works like warming up or stretching before a race.

Meditation is preparation. It prepares me for the rest of my day. The rest of my week. The rest of my month. And the rest of my life.

I know it's working when I can move through my life with a little more ease, and a little less friction.

I know it's working when I see myself starting to respond to life in slightly different ways. In the moments when I am not meditating.

I know it's working when I become conscious of how I am changing.

That forced vacation in Mexico gave me the gift of a lifetime. The experiment of daily meditation continues ten years later for me and I can't imagine living without it.

And that is how I unlearned darkness.

EXPERIMENT REFLECTIONS

Meditation is preparation for life. It's not about the experience while sitting cross legged on a yoga mat, but how it changes my responses in daily life off the mat.

Consistency in meditation builds resilience and helps navigate life with less friction and more ease.

The journey of meditation is deeply personal, evolving through continuous practice and with the support of a like-minded community.

UNLEARNING DISTRACTION

FIVE YEARS WITHOUT EMAIL ON MY PHONE

> So many people walk around with a mean-
> ingless life. They seem half-asleep, even when
> they're busy doing things they think are im-
> portant. This is because they're chasing the
> wrong things.
>
> -Morrie Schwartz

I was spending the evening with fellow entrepreneurs who had successfully navigated the ups and downs of the tech industry we had helped create. As plates of food came and went, conversation flowed from the predictable topic of business to the unsettling topic on all our minds: tech addiction.

I'd spent years uncomfortably addicted to my devices. The irony was clear to me, given that I'd started a technology business. But that was partly *why*. It's like opening a bakery and developing a sweet tooth you just can't shake.

I was constantly spinning plates in my business, trying to find solutions for every problem, and fixing anything that went wrong. In the early years, I kept three smartphone devices on me in order to demo my business's products and to feed my tech addiction.

Email in particular was highly addictive for me. Even when I tried to be disciplined, I always broke. Email was like walking around with a bag of popcorn, constantly stuffing my face. It was not healthy.

The dangling promise of that dopamine hit, though, was often too much to resist. The anticipation of someone sending me a message led me to obsessive inbox checking, even when there was nothing there.

I couldn't sleep well.

I couldn't eat a meal without checking my email.

I couldn't sit through a date without sneaking a peek at my inbox.

Frankly, it made me feel important. I was reacting constantly to the needs of other people, which fed my ego, even if I couldn't admit it to myself.

But it also felt like work. It wasn't the individual actions, but rather their cumulative effect. I felt like I was always working.

Finally, a turning point came. I'd had enough sleepless nights and restless days. I wanted to own technology instead of being owned by it. I needed control.

And so, a new experiment emerged: I took email off my phone.

After studying software engineering and several years into running a successful tech business, I made the choice to disconnect from technology. I had no idea how much that decision would transform my relationship with devices forever.

Society talks a lot about disconnecting from technology.

But talking about it is one thing; actually doing it is another.

I didn't tell anyone I had taken email off my phone—a recurring trend in my experiments. I wanted to see what would happen, and if anyone would notice.

After a day of not having email on my phone, no one said anything. I was surprised. After a week, no one had noticed yet. I was curious. After a month: still no response. I was in.

But *I* was noticing all kinds of things. I felt better and slept better than I had in years. My conversations were deeper and more grounded. When I did have to solve a problem, I came to it with fresh energy and insight. Remarkably, I was doing a *better* job running my business. I was no longer reacting, but now responding.

At the five-year mark of having no email on my phone while being CEO of a growing tech business, I concluded the experiment because I was no longer addicted. During those five years, not a single person had noticed or complained about my responsiveness. Not once.

As a tech addict, technology threw me into a state of hyper-alertness. My reactive mind was constantly scanning, processing, and triaging the world around me. Post addiction, I was operating from a more strategic mode where I found more space.

With fewer hours eaten up by obsessive checking and responding to email, I began to spend more time connecting in real life. Activities like yoga, long walks, showers, countryside drives, writing, or simply cooking a meal are some of my favorite means of disconnecting. These moments often yield the most value, both for myself and others. They create the right conditions for finding clarity.

Opting out of the prevailing culture was challenging, frequently placing me in inconvenient situations. However, this trade-off was crucial over those five years as I recalibrated my relationship with devices.

Disconnecting from my day-to-day lifestyle, routine, and habits started with choosing to unplug 100 percent from business, without exception.

Whether I was checking my device every day, every hour, or every ten minutes, my reactive mode was being triggered. The simple act of picking up my phone disconnected me momentarily from whatever I was doing, jolting me into a state of alertness. What I came to realize was that I had become addicted to those constant *ding*s.

This led to my next experiment: to completely disconnect

from business while on vacation. Where Europeans do this as status quo, the North American status quo is to stay "lightly" connected while away. As some put it, going on vacation is simply responding to emails with better weather and a better view.

I had the perfect chance to try out this experiment on my next vacation: a family trip to India, both for a cousin's wedding and to experience its touristic wonders. While I was born and raised in Canada, my parents, originally from India, went to great lengths to ensure that my sister and I could immerse ourselves in our culture, cuisine, and community. This trip offered an ideal opportunity for a complete disconnection from devices, given the constant novelty and rich experiences at every turn.

I did it and despite at first feeling foreign, I quickly found the peace that arises from being present with the people and place that I am.

After that first vacation where I disconnected completely for two weeks, a distinct and unpleasant feeling arose upon my return: disappointment.

There were not as many emails, issues, questions, and fires to be put out as I'd expected. What I learned from this experiment was that **I am not as important as I think I am.** The world could go on—and my business did go on just fine—without me.

Then came a second, more pleasant feeling: freedom. And a growing realization that not only did my business not suffer when I stepped away from it—it actually prospered.

In truth, my businesses now can't afford for me *not* to disconnect while away. Why? That disconnection allows me to reconnect to the things that matter. It's in this state that I can problem-solve, think, and innovate. There's an opening to come up with my best ideas and find my inspiration.

Creative insights have been critical to my success. They are the "eureka!" moments I crave but rarely have while connected to devices. The thing about creative insights is that they cannot be forced—they come when they come, spontaneously and unpredictably. There is no email, Facebook message, blog post, or YouTube video that is the source of creative insight actionable in my life. **Actionable inspiration is ignited from within.**

Disconnecting from day-to-day work helps cultivate a state of mind that lends itself to creativity. My thinking brain gets a break, letting my insightful brain flourish. Plenty of thoughts are still directed toward my businesses, but in a far more strategic—and valuable—way. The creative insights naturally arise, as deep down there is a part of me that is aware of the problems that need to be solved.

In any business with global clients and ambitious growth expectations, issues will come up. This is a reality. But without me there every minute of every day, I witness my teams step up and show leadership by finding solutions. Seeing people grow in this way is rewarding—not just for me, but for them. They sense my trust and faith in them, and they feel capable and empowered.

Connection has been a powerful theme in my life—and yet it's one that I have often taken for granted. I think I'm more connected than ever, but in many ways, the opposite is true.

Connections with people, places, experiences, knowledge, nature, and most importantly, myself, help me feel grounded, inspired, and focused. But I have learned that, ironically, those connections often start with disconnecting.

As a leader, I felt responsible to set a positive example for the people who work with me. Constantly disrupting the personal lives of my team and clients by sending them emails they will (unfortunately) feel obliged to read and respond to 24/7 sets a terrible example. The cost of burnout of even a single team member is too high. They become unproductive, less efficient, and need more time away to recover. Letting that email wait until the next morning is a smart business decision.

It's also a smart decision for my emotional and mental health. My early years as an entrepreneur were spent tricking myself into thinking, *I'll rest once these emails are answered*. But the stream of incoming requests never stops. The more emails I write, the more I'll receive. It's a loop, and when my brain was in a reactive mode, the loop continued to be fed.

Spoiler alert: disconnecting from tech is not as scary as it sounds. In my experience, everyone benefits—friends, family, colleagues, employees. The steps to a more disconnected life are shockingly simple. In my case, one choice flowed naturally into another.

After resetting my relationship with email on my phone and becoming comfortable enough to fully unplug while on vacation, I soon stumbled on my next experiment in how to disconnect.

Again focused on email, this one was to unsubscribe. For this experiment, I had the idea to set up an email filter that removed from my inbox any email with the word "unsubscribe" in it.

Once I did this, all the spam emails, unwanted newsletters I hadn't signed up for—even the newsletters I *had* signed up for—vanished to a sub folder. I couldn't believe how much time and space it opened up. Every one or two weeks, I scan this sub folder to make sure I haven't missed something important (I rarely have). It was such a simple experiment that has stuck with me years later to this day.

Before these experiments began, back when I still checked my email upon waking, every morning was hijacked by reacting to whatever happened the night before. Now, my morning routine is a source of energy and excitement for the day ahead. I'm able to be more consistent with daily meditation, journaling, yoga, and reading. The day begins in a good place: positive and upbeat. I give myself time and space to process everything inside, connecting to my internal needs before facing the external needs. As a single person who doesn't yet have kids, this is obviously a privilege I recognize I won't have forever.

Making a deliberate decision to disconnect has been transformative. Every morning is a new opportunity to make this choice again for me.

And that is how I unlearned distraction.

EXPERIMENT REFLECTIONS

Technology addiction often stems from a culture that prioritizes constant connectivity. Finding balance requires proactive disconnection.

Email and constant notifications act like a bag of popcorn, endlessly consuming attention. Establishing hard boundaries with technology is essential.

Real freedom is found in being present and engaging deeply with the world around me, rather than through screens and digital distractions.

UNLEARNING FEAR

FOUR DEATH DEFYING JUMPS

The constant assertion of belief is an indication of fear.

-Krishnamurti

It was my first solo vacation. My romantic relationship wasn't in a great place anymore. The experiment with anti-consumerism had recently begun, so had my experiment with committing to meditation. Changes were starting to appear on the surface, as something deep within me had shifted.

I needed some space to process the changes in myself and as a result, in my romantic relationship. So, I went to Costa Rica on one day's notice for a weeklong vacation. While I had no plan for the vacation, I had a plan to temporarily disconnect for the week from my relationship, my business, my devices, and my growing anxiety that something had to change.

I landed at the airport, took a cab into the capital city, San José, and walked into a random hotel, where I stayed for one night. Struggling to find vegetarian food with my phone off, I just wasn't feeling the city vibe.

The next day, I went back to the airport and took another flight, a domestic one to the west coast of the country, to a town called Nosara. It was one of the smallest planes I'd been on; the kind where there were only six passengers. When the solo pilot buckled up and moved his seat forward, I suddenly had more leg room.

During the forty-minute flight, the plane was still below

the clouds. I could see Costa Rica's beautiful landscapes and rainforests from up high.

The white-haired American next to me, super tanned and wearing shorts, was quick to strike up a conversation with me. He asked where I was staying; I told him I had no idea. He asked who was picking me up from the airport; I told him nobody. I'd take a cab.

He laughed at me. As he shook his head and smiled, he said, "This isn't one of those airports, my friend. There are no cabs."

When I floated the idea that I'd walk, he told me it was impossible. The airport was in the middle of nowhere.

"Don't worry," he said. "I got you."

When I asked him for suggestions on where to stay, he asked what I was into, and I told him yoga. He flashed a knowing grin.

His station wagon was parked at the airport. Bumping along in the passenger seat was when it became apparent there were no paved roads in this town.

My new friend explained that the locals had stopped the city from building any infrastructure to avoid being over-crowded with tourists like us. He then dropped me off at a beautiful yoga hotel close to the beach and drove away.

The hotel only had shared rooms, and only one bed available. Of course, my roommate was a Canadian. Forty-year-old Troy, a firefighter from Toronto, was there to surf.

The hotel was connected to a yoga studio, provided only vegetarian food, and was the perfect setup for a self-guided retreat. This time it was in English, unlike the first retreat I'd done a few months earlier in Mexico.

I took two or three daily yoga classes, learned how to surf, connect with interesting travelers over meals, and meditated a lot.

Day four into the weeklong solo retreat, while sitting in meditation one morning, a question came up. What am I scared of?

An answer shot up immediately. Heights. I had been scared of heights my whole life. And from a deeply meditative state, I inquired within, Where did this fear of heights come from?

I began to reflect back to different childhood experiences. However it was difficult to pinpoint a traumatic experience around heights.

A new question arose: Was I born scared of heights? My deep inner wisdom answered immediately. No.

At that point, logic joined the party in my mind. I didn't know when, where, or why I had acquired this fear of heights. But if the fear had been acquired, then maybe it could be disposed of. I was two months into my minimalism experiment at this point, so this idea of disposing of things was becoming familiar.

After searching for the source of this fear and not being able to locate it, I made a choice.

I hadn't been born with it, it wasn't mine; therefore, I could choose to let it go. So, I let it go. It was a ninja mind trick I was convinced might just work.

When I got up from the meditation, I thought, I'm no longer scared of heights. A smile of satisfaction appeared on my face. As I walked toward the communal eating area, I felt like I'd just done mind surgery on myself. And then my wisdom spoke again. This time it said, Prove it.

The universe works in beautiful and unexpected ways. Minutes later, an excited woman walked up to me in the lunch area, grabbed my arms, and shouted, "I just went ziplining! It was amazing. You have to try it."

There I was, smiling, because only moments ago, something deep inside me had said I needed to prove my fear of heights was gone. If this woman had said that to me even a day earlier, I would've dismissed it. But at that moment, I had no choice but to say yes.

I showed up at the zipline spot the next morning. Twenty people milled about—some couples, some families, a mix of old and young. They loaded us all into the back of a truck, and we started driving up a mountain. A very tall mountain.

As we got higher and higher, I noticed my stomach start to develop the familiar sensations of fear. My mind was saying, You're not scared of heights. You're not scared of heights. You're not scared of heights. My stomach was saying, You are scared. You are scared. You are scared.

At the top, they gave us the tutorial on how to put the harness on and other safety instructions. All twenty of us were lined up in a row, listening attentively.

When the instructor asked who would like to go first, half the group took a step forward. The other half, which included me, took a step back. We all looked at each other and laughed. It was clear who the daredevils were, and who the scaredy-cats were.

One by one, all the daredevils started to go. Then there

was a long, awkward pause. Of the ten of us who were left, none of us wanted to go. We were all scared. *Really* scared.

A few of the scaredy-cats found the courage and went. I then tricked myself into thinking, I just need to walk to where the instructor is, ten feet away. I didn't think of the mountain I would be gliding down. Keeping my head down, without looking forward, I told myself all I had to do was walk ten feet. And I did just that.

The first zipline was half a mile long—one of the longest ziplines in Costa Rica. It was also one thousand feet in the air, a powerful height, stretching over sea and rainforest.

I was holding onto the handles of the harness for dear life when the instructor gave me the dreaded push, and my descent began.

On instinct, my eyes closed and my mouth started yelling the mantra, "I was not born scared of heights! I was not born scared of heights! I was not born scared of heights!" Over and over, for the entire half mile. My eyes were closed throughout; I did not see a thing.

When I felt the ground under my feet, I opened my eyes and realized I'd made it to the other side. I was in shock; I couldn't believe I'd done it. Thankfully, it was now over.

Another instructor, staring patiently at me, said, "Congratulations! You just did the first of thirteen."

My jaw dropped. I stood there, blinking in the bright Costa Rican sun, thinking, *What? I have to do this twelve more times?*

On the next line, my eyes stayed open. Instead of yelling the mantra, *I was not born scared of heights,* my body decided to hold its breath. I was still gripping the handles very tightly, but I made it.

On the next one, my grip was a little less tight—and I began to breathe. The next one, I didn't hold anything; I trusted the harness. During the next one, my body no longer crunched into a ball but extended in the air, like the others were doing. On the next one, I took a running start instead of having to be pushed, which gave me more speed. The adrenaline rush was building as my body flew over the forest.

Then I saw the woman next to me, who was kind of cute. "Hey," I said. "Do you want to do this next one together?" She agreed, so we ziplined in tandem, feet interlocked, smiling and laughing at one another.

It was time for the last line. I waited for everybody else to go. The adrenaline was really pumping inside of me by now, and I had an idea that scared me. The last instructor came and told me to go.

My response was, "I want to do this one together, and upside down."

He paused. He smiled. He nodded.

He gave me brief instructions. We stepped back, locked hands, took a running start—and flipped completely upside down as our feet left the cliff. Facing down toward the valley a thousand feet below us, we began to spin each other, doing circus tricks as if we were hanging upside down from a trapeze. Everybody was cheering wildly for us as we landed on the other side.

The smile on my face was massive. The smile in my heart was even bigger. I had gone from a place of extreme fear to completely owning it. I went from fear to fun. I had proven it to myself: I was no longer scared of heights.

The experiment to turn fear to fun continued. A few months later I was with Ray, a close friend from university who, like me, had also been scared of heights. Hearing about my experiment, he said yes to the next leg of the adventure.

We signed up for a tourist attraction in Toronto called the EdgeWalk, where we would walk in a circle along the top of the CN Tower, once the tallest building in the world.

Today, it's still the tallest building in the world that a person can stand on top of.

Noticing the fear we both were feeling, when it was time for the group to go, Ray and I waited to go last. We were both scared. We finally went out, and within minutes were leaning over the edge.

The exercise was called Superman. Standing on the edge of a grill, my body supported only by two harnesses behind me, I leaned forward, looking out. I couldn't see the harnesses behind me, though, so I was just hanging there, overlooking the whole city. The physical sensation of adrenaline was intense. The thoughts were wild, leaning over the entire city with nothing between me and the ground.

And I loved it. They had to ask me three times to get down at the end. I wanted to stay there and hang out, literally, on top of the world as long as I could.

A couple of months later, the experiment to challenge my fear of heights continued. I had a week free in my calendar and took a spontaneous trip. I woke up on a Saturday morning, opened my laptop, and went to the Air Canada website to help me decide where to go. Then I opened Google Maps and started playing around with it, to see what places might trigger some excitement.

After moving the map from Asia to South America, I came across the Bahamas. I noticed a spark inside. There was a yoga ashram in the Bahamas that I'd heard about. I knew that's where I wanted to go, but not for a whole week. I looked at what was on the way to the Bahamas and saw Miami. Done. I booked a flight and left for the airport immediately.

As the plane began its descent into Miami, an unexpected thought arose: This would be a safe place to go skydiving. Still on the runway, I pulled out my phone, turned off airplane mode, typed in "skydiving" on Google Maps, and called the first place that showed up. I booked an appointment for the next morning from the comfort of my airplane seat.

I awoke to a stormy day—a rare occurrence in Miami at that time of the year. My first thought was, The universe is telling me not to jump out of a plane today. The skydiving place agreed. When I called, they told me they weren't doing any jumps that morning but to stay tuned. "If things clear up," they said, "we'll give you a call."

I felt relieved. Until the afternoon when my phone rang—and I knew exactly who it was.

"Okay," they said. "You can come now."

The waiting room was full of other nervous people like me. A giant Turkish man came up to me and said, "We're gonna jump together." I asked him how many times he'd done it, and he said, "Oh, it's my first time." Classic sky-diver humor—and I totally fell for it.

When he saw the genuine fear in my eyes, he put his hand on my shoulder. "Don't worry," he said. "I've done this ten thousand times."

I boarded yet another small tinfoil plane, just big enough for the pilot and the two of us who were jumping in tandem with our respective instructors. The other person was even more nervous than I was, so out of kindness, I offered to go first. I felt I had momentum with this experiment; I was on a roll and still had something left to prove.

A familiar mantra began to play in my head: *I'm not scared of heights. I'm not scared of heights. I'm not scared of heights.* When the plane started to lift above the clouds, I turned to the instructor excitedly and flashed the thumbs-up signal for "let's do it." He showed me the altitude on his watch, which was at 5,000 feet, then told me we were going to 10,000.

Fear and panic rushed over me, and I had no choice but to meditate. I closed my eyes, centered myself and, despite the altitude, grounded myself.

I began to let go. To detach from life. To tell myself that this might be it for me. The end. I felt at peace with that thought. In those few moments, I felt at peace with my life, detaching from it all.

We were now at 10,000 feet. The door opened—and then we jumped out of the plane. Technically, we rolled. The next thing I knew, I was looking at the sky. Not at the ground. I started to freak out and began yelling at the top of my lungs. And then we turned. Now we were looking at the ground, and it was a beautiful, beautiful day. We were still in free fall, gravity drawing us toward the earth. I was still yelling loudly into the wind.

After about twenty seconds, I got tired of yelling, so I stopped. At which point I realized, Wow. This is way more fun when I'm yelling. So, I began to yell again, this time on purpose. The first time was unconscious; the second time was conscious.

Again, I loved it.

I thought back to that first meditation in Costa Rica, where I said to myself, I'm not scared of heights. The memories flowed through me—from ziplining thirteen times, to the tower walk in Toronto where I'd hung out on top of the world, and all the way to this moment, as I floated back down to earth. This was the pinnacle. I had experimented with my fear and found fun as a result.

There are two types of fears in life. Those that keep me living; and those that keep me from living. By bringing awareness and intention to my fears, I felt some agency and choice as I no longer blindly assumed they were mine to keep forever.

And that is how I unlearned fear.

EXPERIMENT REFLECTIONS

True courage involves embracing vulnerability and letting go of the belief that I need to try and control every outcome.

Facing fears directly and repeatedly builds inner strength and resilience.

Trusting in the unknown opens up new possibilities and can lead to profound personal growth.

UNLEARNING CONTROL

ONE MYSTERY TRIP TO AN UNDISCLOSED LOCATION

> *When we are no longer able to change a situation, we are challenged to change ourselves.*
> -Viktor Frankl

It was early December when the question arose while I was meditating one Saturday morning: What will I do for the end-of-year holiday?

My sister had gotten married that year, so she was busy with her in-laws. My parents had their own plans. There was no family gathering or celebration on the calendar. Meanwhile, I'd been traveling every week for business all year long, and the idea of planning a trip or vacation felt effortful and heavy.

During that morning meditation, I found a dose of inspiration. This year, I would experiment with something spontaneous.

Without giving it much thought, I called up my friend Jen. I didn't know Jen super well, but we'd kept in touch since our university days and recently connected when she was visiting New York. She was top of mind.

"Hey Jen," I said nervously. "I want you to pick a place for me to go alone on vacation for the holidays—and not tell me where."

There was a long pause on the other end of the line. "Are you serious?" she asked.

"Yes," I said. "You don't have to do it, but I thought of you. I wanted to ask if you'd be game."

Another long pause. "Are you sure?"

Again, the answer was yes—and that she was free to say no. Silence. I sat there, patiently waiting for her response.

Finally, it came. "Okay," she said. "I'll do it." Then she hung up, and I decided to get on with my day.

An hour later, Jen called me back. "I only have one question for you," she said. "What's off limits?"

I smiled. This was clearly the right friend to pick for this experiment. Thinking out loud, I said, "I don't want to end up in prison. And I've got a bad knee." That was my way of signaling: Don't send me to Machu Picchu. Lastly: "Nothing to do with drugs."

That was it. Three restrictions.

"Got it," she said. "Consider it done."

I got off the phone and didn't think much more about it. I was busy wrapping up the year for my business and was also in the middle of a nine-month yoga teacher training program. My New York life was active. I didn't hear from Jen and didn't think to reach out. I kind of forgot about the experiment once I set it in motion.

One week later, an email from Jen arrived. In the subject line: "Packing List." Nothing in the body of the email—just a document attachment. It was four pages long.

Jen and I weren't close. She wasn't aware that at that moment in my life, I was an extreme minimalist. After years of not buying a single thing and sleeping on other people's couches, I had no possessions; I'd moved to New York with a carryon suitcase. Oh boy, I thought. Here we go. I opened the document, then quickly closed it. It felt overwhelming.

The next day at my yoga teacher training, I said to a close friend May, "Hey, I'm taking a trip and need a few things." She asked where I was going, and when she heard about my experiment, she flipped out excitedly.

May was a New Yorker who'd lived in the city her whole life. She was a tough cookie—and very encouraging of my experiment. "I've got the backpack," she said. "And a flashlight for you. And that's about it." She told me where to buy a few things, and I gathered the minimum supplies for this spontaneous trip: a backpack with four or five days' worth of shirts, pants, a bathing suit, and lots of socks.

A few days later, I flew back to Toronto and went to my parents' house for a few hours to see my family and tell them I was leaving on a trip. My mom thought I was ridiculous. My dad didn't quite understand. "So where are you going?" he asked a few times. Every time I told him the same thing: I had no idea. My sister kept asking, "Can I come?" I told her no; this was just for me.

That evening, I was at Jen's house. I'd never been to her place before. As she greeted me at her door, she confidently said, "Let's take my dog for a walk," so we walked to the park. I was jittery with nerves, and she could feel it. She was about to send me anywhere in the world—and I had no idea where.

"How are your parents?" she said.

"You've never met my parents," I snapped back.

"How are your sister and brother?"

"I just have a sister," I said.

The tension was thick. I was anxious, and she was trying to make small talk to play with me. But as we walked, I started to calm down. We had dinner at her place and started digging into some intellectual conversation, which was a helpful distraction. All the while, in the back of my mind I'm thinking, Let's get on with this.

Finally, I turned to her and said, "Is it time?"

She looked at her watch, then grinned. "It's time."

"Where am I going?"

"I'm not telling you," she said.

She reached for a stack of envelopes on the chair beside her, then slid them across the table very dramatically like a drug deal. "Don't open them yet," she growled. She was clearly enjoying her mobster persona. She told me each envelope was dated, and to not open any of them until I got to my final destination.

The Uber came. He asked where I was going, and I told him the truth: I had no idea. He stopped talking to me, and a little bit later, we arrived at the airport. Part of the experiment was to disconnect fully, so I turned off my phone in the Uber.

I've been to the airport hundreds of times, if not a thousand, but I've always known where I was going. To this day, that was the only time I'd gone to the airport with no idea. I approached the Air Canada check-in counter and handed the attendant my passport.

"Where are you going today?" she said.

"I don't know."

She blinked at me, unimpressed. "What do you mean, you don't know?"

"A friend booked this for me as a surprise," I blurted out.

There was a long pause. She looked puzzled. "That's very irresponsible," she said firmly. "What if you need a visa?" Without thinking, I said I was Canadian, and she acknowledged my point. Canadians don't need visas to go to many places in the world. Everyone will happily take us.

She grabbed my passport, annoyed, and looked up my flight using it. Her facial expression changed in an instant. "Oh, you have a very nice friend. I wish I had a friend like yours. Are you sure you don't want to know where you're going?"

"Yes," I responded nervously. She looked me straight in the eyes and could see I was serious.

"Hold on," she said. "I'll be right back."

At that point, I started to feel more nervous. She returned with a colleague; he asked me all the same questions to reconfirm the story, and I gave all the same answers. Finally, they turned to each other—and smiled.

"Okay," said the original attendant. "We'll play ball with you."

I was starting to get excited. She told me I had three flights to take. I sighed. She handed me the first boarding pass, which was to Copenhagen. The flight left in an hour.

"We're going to put the second and third boarding passes in envelopes and seal them," she said. "Only open them when you absolutely have to open them. We're also going to track you, and our marketing team will want to talk to you once you're back."

We exchanged phone numbers. She told me she'd been working behind the counter for twenty-five years and never seen anybody do this before. I laughed and said, "I like to be the first."

I slept for most of the red-eye to Copenhagen. All the while I'm thinking, "Gosh, Jen. I'm Canadian. Please don't keep me in Scandinavian countries—I've seen enough winters!"

I landed, deplaned, and stood in the Copenhagen terminal with my backpack. I took a deep breath and opened the second boarding pass. I was going to Bangkok in two hours.

By the time I got to Thailand, I'd gone twenty-four hours without eating anything, because Thai Airways didn't have any vegetarian options. I was famished and overwhelmed. I had a couple hundred dollars in cash, a credit card, my phone off, and a backpack with four days of clothes. There I was, roaming the Bangkok airport, thinking, what's going to happen?

When I opened the third boarding pass, it said: Denpasar.

I stared at it. My flight for Denpasar was leaving in three hours, and all I could think was: Where is Denpasar?!

In that moment, I learned two things. One: Boarding passes don't have countries on them. Two: boarding passes don't show arrival times. Without those two pieces of information, I had no idea where this was. And I was fully disconnected, with no desire to turn my phone back on. I scanned the computer screens in the airport, all to no avail. Denpasar could be anywhere. I assumed it was somewhere remote in Thailand (it was not).

I started to meditate and journal, trying to quiet my mind and capture my experience of the experiment. When I boarded the plane, I still had no idea where it was going. I sat down, relatively calm, noticing the full range of emotions that were coming up.

And then came the moment of truth, unexpectedly. An hour into the flight, the woman sitting next to me tapped my shoulder and said, "Have you been to Bali before?"

I stared at her, eyes wide open, quietly processing what she'd said. I'm going to Bali, I thought. I felt a rush of excitement and relief. I smiled. "No," I told her. "My first time."

At the airport, I opened the first envelope from Jen. It was a printout from Expedia with a hotel reservation in Kuta, the city where the Denpasar airport is. The hotel reservation was only for one night. There were no other instructions, just a hotel reservation printout. I found my way there and, needless to say, slept like a rock.

At breakfast the next morning, I met an older Australian couple named Pete and Carla. They were celebrating Pete's sixty-fifth birthday—and they happened to be Bali experts. It was their eighth visit. They absolutely ate up the story of my journey over the past thirty-six hours. They wanted to know every little detail.

Then I pulled out the second envelope and said, "Pete, would you like to open this for me?"

He loved it. Inside was a hotel reservation in a small town two hours away. Pete and Carla helped me figure out how to get there.

From then on, I'd show up in each new place, opening an envelope every day or two that told me where to go and sometimes what to do. A few of the envelopes were purposefully empty.

It was an *Eat Pray Love* meets *Amazing Race* adventure, filled with adventure sports, a vacation romance, getting sick twice, discovering a love of dance, deep spiritual connection, new business inspiration, and more.

I expected to be gone for two weeks, but at the two-week mark, the envelopes kept coming. The date of my return trip was a mystery. But three and a half weeks after I'd left Canada, I finally opened an envelope to see a flight for my trip home.

This was an experiment in trust. I had to learn to let go of control.

I had to learn to trust Jen.

I had to learn to trust the many people I would meet.

I had to learn to trust the universe.

I had to learn to trust myself, most importantly.

The lesson was to trust that I had the inner resources and skills to deal with whatever situations might arise. Instead of trying to control my outer world, I could only turn inward. It built strength, resolve and confidence that I am okay and will be okay.

That was the real journey: to put myself in an extreme place of vulnerability that ultimately led to a lot of growth, and a lot of freedom. **The freedom to know that I don't need to know everything, and the freedom that I don't always want to know.**

And that is how I unlearned control.

EXPERIMENT REFLECTIONS

Trust is developed by embracing vulnerability and relying on our inner resources and skills to navigate unfamiliar territory.

Letting go of control and trusting the process can lead to significant experiences that shape my growth and path in life.

The journey of trust is about building confidence in my ability to handle whatever comes my way.

UNLEARNING
STABILITY

THREE DAYS NOTICE TO MOVE COUNTRIES

By replacing fear of the unknown with curiosity, we open ourselves up to an infinite stream of possibility.

-Alan Watts

I was back in Toronto, having moved out of New York. I didn't know how long I'd stay in Canada, but I sensed my next experiment was imminent. There was a growing desire deep within me to leave North America. Or rather, to leave my North American life and identity and challenge myself with something new.

Choosing where to move was not an easy decision. I found myself drowning in options for a few weeks. Hours were spent going down internet rabbit holes, reading travel blogs and expat stories, and asking friends for ideas. The information was endless. Anywhere was possible.

A sense of overwhelm set in. I noticed how big of a distraction this decision was. I was dreaming about it at night, so during the day it was impossible to concentrate on much else. The rest of my life had been put on pause. Now I can see I was experiencing fear. Fear of making the "wrong" decision. Fear of regret.

Unsure what to do, I gave myself some space. I would not think about it or talk about it for a few days. I assumed that, after this break, I would either still want to move—or abandon the idea altogether. This momentary mental break was the best thing I could have done.

It may feel counterintuitive, but when faced with a problem, I like to stop trying to solve the problem

and instead take a break.

It works. This has been my experience time and again. The clarity surfaces once I turn away. Something deeper within me, or bigger than me, is often the source of this clarity.

Day three of my mental break coincided with my birthday. I woke up and sat in my traditional three-hour continuous birthday meditation, a ritual that has stayed with me for nearly a decade.

While I sat there quietly, my mind was anything but quiet. It went everywhere. After a few hours, the question that appeared was: What is important to me, right now? What do I desire in my life right now? What would make my heart sing?

It was not: What is expected of me? What is convenient and easy? What is safe and low risk?

Within seconds, my heart spoke and I listened:

- To live by the water. I have always lived in cities and wanted to live by the ocean for once.

- To have beautiful weather all year long. I grew up in Canada. Enough said.

- To be around nice people. A place that brings out

the kindness of humanity, where I could speak to a stranger in the street and strike up a conversation with ease.

- To be in a place with a relaxed vibe. In other words, a place where people don't primarily identify with what they do and are competing for everything. So, not New York.

- To be within a direct flight of family. To stay connected with their lives.

A smile appeared on my face. My heart began to sing. All fear disappeared, as the reasons *not* to move stopped. I now knew *why* to move—and I was starting to hone in on *where*.

There were about a dozen countries in the world that I had been researching and considering before this clarity appeared. Now there was only one country I felt inspired by.

Portugal.

My meditation timer rang shortly after. I quietly got up, went to my laptop, and immediately booked a one-way ticket to Lisbon. My flight left in three days.

My next experiment had begun. I called it the

one-way-ticket mindset. So much in life asks for a one-way-ticket mindset; this philosophy is bigger than travel. The one-way ticket mindset represents an "all-in" mindset, in which I am choosing to emotionally commit in advance of having all the facts. It involves extreme vulnerability and trust, both of which I had been practicing and cultivating through many of my previous experiments.

When I reflect on the one-way ticket mindset, I realize it might be one I learned before I was born: my parents immigrated to Canada while my mom was eight months pregnant with me. It continued when I left home for university, and was strengthened by the practice of booking several one-way tickets to new places for impromptu vacations. The biggest example was starting and running a business.

Committing the resources of a business to a specific direction, entering partnerships with clients, and choosing to hire someone are all forms of a one-way ticket. Building a meditation practice, starting a new professional role, entering into a romantic partnership, learning a new language, and playing a sport all work best when approached with the one-way-ticket mindset.

These examples—and more in life—all worked better

when I jumped into the deep end rather than only dipping a toe in the water. It requires moving, trusting, and leaping instead of standing still.

And it requires letting go. **By letting go of what *was*, I could make space for what might be.** There was no looking back, no comparison to the past, no safety net of hitting the undo or rewind button.

I intentionally did not research or plan much in the three days between making my decision and hopping on my one-way flight to Portugal. The adventure of not knowing and not planning felt exciting to me.

As I sat on the flight from Toronto to Lisbon, I reflected more deeply about this next chapter in life I was beginning. It's natural to feel fear on a one-way ticket. What if I don't like it? What if it doesn't work? But those questions play most loudly in my head when I *don't* commit to something mentally and emotionally. The easier-said-than-done antidote to this fear is to make another decision in response to the original decision, if it turns out the first choice no longer works.

How much I receive from an experience, opportunity, person, or place is proportional to how much of myself I give to it. The question changes from: "What do I want?" to "What am I willing to give?"

Upon first arriving in Portugal to start my next chapter, I felt nervous. The move was spontaneous. I didn't know a single person in Lisbon, since I hadn't stayed in touch with the people I'd met couchsurfing years earlier. My first few weeks were rough emotionally. With no friends and no connection to the local culture, I felt lost. I discovered many hard truths about this new place I'd decided spontaneously to call home.

After feeling lost in Lisbon a few weeks in, I realized why: I was still acting like a visitor in Europe. I hadn't grounded myself. It was time to commit emotionally to this new place I wanted to call home. And within weeks of that moment, I had a local phone number, bank account, credit card, health card, rental apartment, car, and most importantly, friends. More on how that came to be in the next chapter.

But this, like so many of my choices, was an experiment. I decided I would give myself to this next chapter in life freely and fully. It's an intentional choice to not look back, to not test the waters, to not carry any regret.

Moving to Portugal paved a path for me to not only change my trajectory, but to fall back in love with my life. This was the experiment of a lifetime, packed with opportunities for adventure, growth, and learning.

But **to change my life, I first had to change myself.** This meant changing my expectations, changing my desires and changing my beliefs.

It would be easy to reflect on the beauty of Portugal and all the things that make it a desirable destination to live. And it can be. But in my heart, I feel that any place can be a desirable destination. For each highlight there is a lowlight, no matter where I might be. Anywhere can be magical and inspiring, if I choose to make it so.

A year previously, if someone had told me that a typical morning would involve making celery juice, practicing Portuguese, and going for a dip in the cold Atlantic ocean, I would have laughed.

When I reflect on life in Portugal, I feel grateful. Every few days, I am brought to tears with appreciation for the life I have thanks to the openness to change myself. The richness of friends and community that I enjoy is inspiring for me every day. What was initially foreign quickly became familiar to me, as I moved through my days with more ease and less friction.

In any decision in life, there will be more reasons to *not* do something than to do it. There were countless reasons I shouldn't have moved to Portugal. But I will not share them here, as I don't need to. What matters far more than what my mind fears is what my heart desires.

And that is how I unlearned stability.

EXPERIMENT REFLECTIONS

Embracing curiosity over fear of the unknown can lead to transformative experiences.

Committing myself emotionally to a new environment is key to feeling at home and making meaningful connections.

Every place has potential for magic and inspiration if I choose to see it that way, highlighting the importance of perspective.

UNLEARNING ANXIETY

ONE HUNDRED FRIENDS IN ONE YEAR

> The essentials of human happiness are simple, so simple that sophisticated people cannot bring themselves to admit what it is they really lack.
>
> -Viktor Frankl

I grew up with not many close friends in grade school and high school. I could count on one hand the number of close friends I had until the age of sixteen.

The first reason was that I was quite shy and socially anxious. I was not socially *awkward* but felt nervous in social situations. I learned how to hide it well. I would hide behind my intellect, sticking to topics I was confident about. I would hide it by becoming curious about the other person, having learned that people love to talk about themselves when invited to.

The second reason was that I have a large extended family, and we were very close growing up. There were always so many people around, I didn't feel the need to get out of my comfort zone socially. Once or twice a week, the house was packed and noisy. Dozens of cousins, aunts, and uncles sharing meals, opinions, and laughs. My parents were social creatures and had countless family friends, mostly of Indian origin, like us, living in Ottawa, Canada.

The third reason was my sister. She was a blabbermouth and loved the spotlight. I unknowingly took a lot of comfort and safety in hiding behind her. Since she always took the lead and showed initiative in social situations, I did not have to do very much.

The turning point came at seventeen. Despite my shyness,

I managed to get elected for student government every year in middle school and high school, then student council president in high school.

On the first day of school of my final year, I had to make the morning announcements from the principal's office. My shyness and social anxiety came through that morning as I nervously read from the piece of paper the principal handed me. After the dreadful four minutes were over, the principal turned to me and said, "This isn't going to work."

It was a deer-in-the-headlights moment. I was in silent shock, struggling to process the gravity of what he had just said. He would go on to explain that in my role as student council president, I was expected to be a high-energy, enthusiastic, and excited role model for all 1,600 students in my school. I would be the first voice they heard each morning, and it was my job to inspire them, among many other responsibilities.

In that moment, which I will remember clearly for the rest of my days, I made a choice. I decided to shed my social anxiety and fear of being seen and step into this new role fully. At first it was not easy, but I was motivated and, thankfully, supported. I often think back to that conversation and how the trajectory of my life has changed because of it.

The next year, at university, the friend pool was larger. I got into a relationship with an extroverted woman and ended up meeting a ton of people through her. My closest new friend at university was also extroverted, so my social circle expanded effortlessly.

As I started to step further into my identity as a student leader on campus, I did a lot of networking, building my interpersonal skills through foundational experiences, like the experience I'd had in high school. I built confidence as I communicated with strangers and engaged in stimulating conversations with people I didn't know in social, academic, political, and business contexts.

Fast forward nearly twenty years, when I spontaneously move to Portugal without knowing a single person. One of the first questions people ask me is, "How have you made friends?"

There is so much information in an innocent question. Most often, it is masking a hidden fear or insecurity someone has.

Two years into my Portugal experiment, I had made a *lot* of friends and new connections. Learning how to make friends as an adult has been an experiment in its own right for me—and a highly successful one.

I'm far past the Dunbar number, the theory that suggests there's a cognitive limit on how many social relationships we can maintain at one time (the magical number is 150). I'm hosting small weekly gatherings, and large monthly gatherings. And I love it. Yes, I find the people interesting. More importantly, though, it is a reminder of how far I've come from that kid who had very few friends and was too shy to talk with people he didn't know.

While I grew up identifying as being a shy introvert, I have grown into an outgoing introvert who gets energy from being around the right people, in the right context, with the right intentionality.

I could write an entire book on how to make friends as an adult—and maybe I will. There are known challenges to making friends beyond the obvious school and work circles, and as a foreigner in a new city, country, and continent who was desperate for connection, I had to learn how to make friends.

The first step: deciding to make friends. Sounds simple, but it's true. I had to decide this was important to me and make a conscious commitment to prioritize it. During my school years, I did not make that decision. I chose learning and studying, and I chose family. After university I chose business. That was my priority, and there wasn't much space for anything else. Making friends just wasn't that important to me in those phases in life.

Choosing to prioritize friendship is bigger than it seems at the surface, because it involves making trade-offs. Time, attention, and energy are limited. A conscious trade-off I made was to prioritize my integration into a new environment over growing my North American connections. My Portuguese Whatsapp is on the first screen of my phone; my North American Whatsapp is on the last. This decision to make trade-offs was an important touchstone I will come back to.

Another part of integrating into a new environment is staying open to a new culture, acknowledging the fact that people in this culture wouldn't always behave like the people in Toronto or New York. During my first few days in Lisbon, I took a walking tour of the city. The guide spoke about how the cobblestone streets are dangerous if you walk too fast, which I interpreted as a metaphor for the ethos of Portugal. The streets are a literal reminder to slow down. Most things here move slowly, by design. It's not a defect; it's a feature.

The way Portugal, and Europe in general, operates is different from what I'm used to after living in North America my entire life. Having the benefit of meeting many expats in Portugal, I can see a clear difference between those who, like me, have a bright smile on their faces, and those who have frowns. I believe the difference is that some people have an ability to adapt to a new environment, whereas others have an expectation that the environment will adapt to them.

Step two: emotionally commit. When I had moved to New York long ago, I was introduced to a Canadian who'd been living there for five years. I went to have coffee with her and was a wide-eyed puppy brimming with curiosity. "How does a Canadian move to New York?" I asked. "Do you see yourself living in New York five years from now? Do you see yourself here forever?"

Her response was the most noncommittal answer I have ever heard. She said, "Maybe. I don't know. Let's see how things go. I didn't think I'd be here this long, but I've been saying that for years, so you never know."

In that moment, my energy shifted. I thought, I do not want to be like her. I do not want to come across this uncommitted. I found myself less interested in building a friendship with her, since I didn't know if she was committed to being in New York.

After moving to Lisbon, the digital-nomad capital of the

world, I met many people who were not committed emotionally to being there. And that's fine. It is a personal choice. But noncommitment wasn't for me.

There are signs I looked for that someone is emotionally committed. Did they have a Portuguese phone number? Did they have a bank account and credit card and health insurance? Do they know any Portuguese people? Were they starting to learn a bit of the language? These are small choices, things that cost maybe fifty or a hundred euros, but they signaled, "I am here."

I now believe it is impossible to make friends with people if they're not committed to being in the place we are both in. They're essentially putting up a big sign that says, "I'm not worth investing in."

The reverse is also true.

From the start of my Portugal experiment, I emotionally committed to Portugal. I got a place, a car, a credit card, and a phone number. I started to take language classes and learn basic Portuguese within one month of moving. I gave off clear vibes saying, "I'm here. I'm worth investing in." And people invested in me. They made time and effort for me, and me for them.

To be clear: I'm not perfect at any of these things. Perfection is not the goal. Take language as an example. Am I fluent in Portuguese? No. But I can go to a restaurant, gas station, or grocery store and communicate without having to rely on English. In this, as in all things, I try to keep a beginner's mindset, showing gentleness to myself.

I may be a beginner, but I'm emotionally committed. People sense that, and they lean in.

Step three: stay grounded. Part of the beauty of living in Europe is that it's so cheap and easy to fly around to different countries to enjoy a variety of cultures, climates, languages, and foods. From Lisbon, I can fly anywhere within Europe in a few hours. My first weekend in Portugal, I went to Dublin to see some extended family. The next weekend I went to Italy to see some old friends from Canada who were there for the summer.

Initially, the thrill of being able to jump on a plane and go somewhere for the weekend was amazing. But when I came back from Italy, I found myself sitting on the runway, thinking, What am I doing? I have moved to Portugal not to play European tourist, but to actually live there and start the next chapter of my life.

So, I told myself, I'm not going to leave Portugal. I'm not going to leave until I make friends, feel grounded, and feel settled. And that's what I did. I didn't get on a plane or take any trips for months.

To be honest, it was hard. I had friends across Europe inviting me to see them for a weekend. But staying in the place I lived made all the difference. When new people invited me to an event, gathering, or coffee chat, I didn't have to say, "Thanks, but I won't be here." It's fine to say that once, but if I said it twice, they probably wouldn't invite me a third time. I've been on the other side many times; after I invite someone to something two or three times and they haven't come, I stop inviting them. Commitment to a friendship is a two-way street.

At the start, while I was trying to build momentum and a foundation of connections with new people in a new place, being present and available was absolutely critical. As I gradually brought travel back into my life, I was intentional about when I did it, and how much.

Step four: be authentically interested, which means showing up and doing the things I was interested in. When I was in New York, it was meditation and yoga; I'd go to meditation classes two or three times a week and yoga classes several times a week. I went to Kirtans, spiritual gatherings that included music and chanting. Every day I went to something that was tied to an activity or interest I was personally into at that moment in time. And just by showing up at places that I was genuinely interested in, I would naturally connect with other people who were interested in those same things.

In Lisbon I started to participate in a meetup a new friend was organizing related to life philosophies. The organizer, David, was introduced to me by two different mutual friends living in other parts of the world. The first thing I said to David when I met him was, "You have no choice but to be my friend now."

I also joined a members' club that appealed to creative and entrepreneurial people, where I made many new connections. Showing up to activities that were of interest to me was a joy. It felt fun and effortless. Finding like-minded people with similar interests is a great basis for connection, I learned.

Step five: be shameless about asking people for their numbers. I did this even without always knowing if I wanted to stay in touch. As soon as I felt a connection, I would say, "Hey, would you like to change numbers?" Or, "Can I get your number?" Ten times out of ten, they said yes. I put them in my phone, with a note or two so I could remember who they were, sent them a message to make sure they have my number, and *voila*: the door for potential connection was open.

<u>Step six: say yes.</u> This one was harder but revealed whether I was truly open to making new friends. When I got invited to a gathering or saw an event online that *seemed* interesting, saying yes meant driving, commuting, or taking an Uber. It committed me to showing up without knowing whether it would be a good use of my time.

It was easy to say yes to things that felt safe. i.e., gatherings where I knew lots of people or the host or events where I knew the content or was interested in the topic. It's easy to do the things I like, whether by myself or with other people. But saying yes to opportunities to connect with people when there was incomplete information required a leap of faith.

What's really interesting is that the moral of the story is not, Oh, I've mostly been right and the event was amazing. When I started saying yes, I would often show up to something that, at the time, felt like a waste of time.

Case in point: I went to an introduction to Portuguese class a month after moving. The studio looked terrible; the reviews were horrible. But since it was the only option close to where I was living at the time, I figured I'd check it out.

I knew from the moment I walked in that the reviews were right. The place was uninspiring—it also doubled as a music school. The teacher was incredibly disorganized; he was not even a native Portuguese speaker, and let's just say teaching was not his gift. It couldn't have been a worse class.

But then, across the table, was a South African couple. We all shared a look, one that telegraphed: This is a waste of our time. Afterward, all three of us walked out the door without signing up for the class. Instead, we started chatting. We discovered we had similar interests. Later that week, we went for a hike and really connected. They're some of my closest friends to this day.

If I hadn't said yes to a Portuguese language class that looked horrible—and *was* horrible—I wouldn't have met them. Just saying yes and going to something without expectation, without trying to optimize the experience and make the best use of my time, really opened me up.

Step seven: hosting people, which I know isn't easy for everyone. Hosting is really an invitation to be seen.

Within my first month, I hosted six new friends for dinner. I remember giving a short speech to acknowledge the gravity of the occasion for me. It was my first time inviting people over in this new place I now called home. I ordered Indian takeout food and had everyone over to my Airbnb rental. It was nothing fancy, and that was the point: hosting does not need to be an elaborate affair. It's the intention that matters most.

Inviting people to my home feels like extending an olive branch. It also requires a certain degree of vulnerability because people could say no. But that's exactly why it's so intimate. I'm being vulnerable, inviting people into my home and my world. I'm sharing myself, and that provides a path for connection.

My journey from a shy kid in school to being called the unofficial mayor of Lisbon, because of how many people I now know, involved a lot of experimentation, openness and courage. The returns from feeling connected to the people where I am are tremendous and worth the investment of time and energy.

And that is how I unlearned anxiety.

❋

EXPERIMENT REFLECTIONS

Forming meaningful connections requires intentionality, openness, and vulnerability.

Hosting and inviting others into my space is a powerful act in service of greater connection and intimacy.

The path from shyness to becoming confident socially involved continuous experimentation and courage, at every step in the journey.

UNLEARNING WORK

ONE UNEXPECTED FIRING

One of the symptoms of an approaching nervous breakdown is the belief that one's work is terribly important.

-Bertrand Russell

This chapter could easily be titled How *Not* to Work. I have a lot of experience with this.

My first time working in business was at the age of six. My sister beat me—she was five when we both joined our parents in the family businesses. Our parents were struggling to get their start in Canada as immigrants who had moved from India weeks before I was born. My father was always an entrepreneur, having tried many different ventures in his teens and twenties.

Once he found his stride, he finally landed on something that worked: retail stores. Specifically franchises of Canada Post, the national postal service. That is where I got my start in business. I am grateful for the early exposure my parents gave me. It shaped my confidence and conviction that, one day, I could start a business. And I did, multiple times.

In my teenage years, I had a few attempts at various businesses. Some worked; most didn't. The businesses could have been called nonprofits: they lost money, despite my humble attempts at the age of thirteen. But what mattered more was that I was encouraged by my parents every step of the way.

I took a detour from business for nearly a decade, as I got more interested in student politics and youth leadership.

Little did I know the skills I would learn running organizations through high school and university would give me the foundational skills for leadership and management in business.

The technology business I started at twenty-one and led as Chief Everything Officer for fifteen years became the defining chapter of my professional identity. I felt I had been training for this role for the earlier fifteen years, starting at the tender age of six.

As Chief Everything Officer, I learned a lot about how *not* to work. I made every mistake one could imagine. I ran out of money a few times. Missed payroll twice. Hired and fired countless people. Burned out multiple times. Burned out my team, including close friends. Upset clients. Lost clients. Disappointed investors. Disappointed myself.

Despite a rollercoaster of a journey, I learned only one thing about how to work: to not overly identify with it.

There was a moment, ten years into my CEO journey, when I was ready to give up. I felt I had given it my all intellectually, emotionally and financially. I had put absolutely everything I had to give into the business. Yet, despite being in my early thirties, I had not a single financial asset to my name other than my shares—and they weren't worth much.

Really, the issue was not that the business was not worth much. The issue was that I had linked my identity fully to the business, so *I* was not worth much. I felt like a failure. A difficult pill to swallow.

And then everything changed.

It was April and spring was in the air. I woke up at four in the morning from a vivid dream. In the dream, I was no longer CEO of my business. I had been relieved of my duties, and the business had hired a new CEO to replace me.

I was in a board meeting, sitting around the table with the other board members and shareholders. The new CEO walked in and sat down. He looked familiar. I couldn't believe it: I was the new CEO.

In this dream, I had fired myself—and then hired myself. But I was hired not as a founder to start the business, but as a turnaround CEO to *fix* the business. As the new CEO, this was no longer my failing business. It was no longer my failure to own. The past baggage was not mine to deal with. It was day one for me. I parachuted in to turn this business around.

Immediately I saw this dream for what it was: my subconscious creating another of my famous experiments to see if

I could turn the business around.

The next few years were the stuff business school case studies are made of. I made thirty major changes, swiftly and without hesitation. Each one required a major shift in the team, the products, the clients, the investors, the board, the brand, and more. I spun those plates hard, well, and fast. I pivoted the business without any attachment to what it meant to me.

I no longer identified with the business. I felt a level of detachment that created a clearer sense of objectivity. By taking space to see the cold hard facts about the business, it was obvious what had to change.

Instead of moaning and groaning about feeling like a failure, I focused on how to run a successful business without the emotion of identifying with its outcome. And it worked. It really worked. This was the secret to my success that took over a decade to uncover.

The size of the business more than doubled within eighteen months of the night I had that dream; profits tripled and the trajectory shifted in a material way. The business had a new life, and it continues to be wildly successful beyond my dreams today with hundreds of clients in nearly every corner of the world.

Finally feeling satisfied as CEO, I decided to hire another CEO. This time, the new CEO was *not* me. Another experiment.

For the business, this was an important milestone: it was no longer to be led by the person who started it fifteen years earlier. No longer founder-led and founder-run, the change in leadership was a clear vote of confidence in the team and the clients. As a significant shareholder in the business, I was ready to make the change because I believed it would lead to greater growth. I was ready to pass the baton onto a more capable leader for the next stage of the business.

For me, this marked another profound shift in my professional identity. Since founding the business in my early twenties, I had been known to my external world as a CEO. This was no longer the case.

Like most professionals, I've spent years building my career with a high level of enthusiasm, excitement, and energy. Naturally, I have identified closely with what I do. For the majority of my adult life, when meeting someone new, whether at a business gathering, a party, or even on a date, the first or second question was always, "What do you do?"

If my identity were visualized as a pie chart, the pie would have had no slices at the beginning of my career: my business was my whole identity, which is often the case for entrepreneurs starting out. Over time, though, the pie has been sliced as my interests and passions have evolved and diversified. Other slices were added when I became an uncle, a meditation teacher, a mental health advocate, and an expat living in Portugal.

That dream I had relieved me from carrying the load and burden of my past disappointments and gave me a fresh start. This fresh start had less to do with protecting some image that I had of myself as a CEO and more to do with focusing on what was most likely to work with the business.

Often the stress that comes from work comes from the implications of the work on one's identity, versus the actual work itself. **As I learn to identify less with what I do, I find that I am more effective in what I do.**

And that is how I unlearned work.

EXPERIMENT REFLECTIONS

Work became more successful and satisfying, and less stressful, when I detached from my strong identity with it.

Balancing work with personal life enhances overall well-being and effectiveness with work itself.

Understanding that work serves my goals in life, and does not define my worth in life, led to a healthier relationship with work.

UNLEARNING BUSYNESS

ONE RADICAL MINDSET SHIFT

It did not really matter what we expected
from life, but rather what life expected from
us.

-Viktor Frankl

One morning, while I was staying in my parents' home in Toronto, I was rushing to prepare a morning smoothie for breakfast. I had the morning ritual down to a precision sport. The defrosted frozen fruit, the perfect amount of almond milk, the hemp, chia and flax seeds, the amount of time the blender would be on. Not being in my kitchen though, that morning I miscalculated the power of the blender and the size of the container. I had to run it for a few extra seconds. And that threw off the rest of my morning, it seemed.

My dad turned to me in the kitchen and innocently said, "You look like you're in a rush."

Without hesitation, without even looking his way, I snapped, "Yes, I have to go meditate now and I'm hungry."

It was only once I walked upstairs to my sister's old bedroom—which I had commandeered as my makeshift meditation studio—and sat down in her chair that I caught up to the irony of my response.

As I shared with the meditation group I was leading on Zoom that morning, the rushing to meditation and yoga classes was a classic New York phenomenon: unique to the hustle and bustle of the environment, and one I had experienced far too many times to admit. The desire to optimize the mundane and squeeze efficiency out of the boring routines was how I had found greater meaning. Now I've learned that rushing to slow down had less to do with New York—and more to do with me.

The comedy of rushing to slow down prompted me to experiment with how to *be*, versus how to *do*. First, I had to understand why I have this strong impulse to *do*.

Doing continuously takes a toll. On my body, my mind, and most of all, my emotions.

A teacher once shared with me, "You have nowhere to go, you are always on your way." This teaching has served me well to help loosen the tight grip my mind has on always expecting to be fill every moment with doing. Always expecting to be *doing* something. Anything.

I learned to be productive from my mom. She is an *Energizer Bunny* who bounces around between cooking in the kitchen, learning from YouTube videos, painting landscapes, working in the garden, annoying my father with endless commentary, talking with my sister on the phone, and her never-ending struggle of trying to connect her phone to her printer. (I had strong doubts this was possible—and was glad to be proven wrong.)

When I complete a task, be it doing the dishes, writing a blog post, or even sitting in meditation, my brain releases the famous dopamine hormone that leads to a pleasurable sensation. From what I've heard and read, the experience of consuming alcohol, drugs, Netflix, or Instagram also releases dopamine in the brain. It literally feels good to be productive and—no surprise—it becomes addictive. It certainly has for me.

The Western culture has also led me to believe that being productive is a good thing, for both individuals and the collective. Productivity leads to progress for all of humanity—and it's required, right? I am expected to live a productive life. But here's my question: Is it required at *all* moments? And is there a cost to always trying to be productive?

The week after I rushed to meditation practice, I went on a walk in my parents' neighborhood. It's an unbelievably quiet and peaceful area. So, what did I do? I took my phone out and started calling friends. After three different attempts met with voicemail greetings, I put my phone back in my pocket—and lifted my head.

I heard the sound of the wind dancing with the trees. I saw the brightness of the sun illuminate every inch of the neighborhood without discrimination. I watched two squirrels playing and chasing one another. And then I felt a smile of a different variety appear on my face. This one was not triggered from a dopamine release in my brain. It was inspired by a deep connection with reality, with nature, and with the present moment.

The desire to feel productive can be superseded with another desire. The desire to connect more deeply with this present moment, and all of its peace and suffering. To connect begins with a pause, so that I can see, hear, and observe reality as it is, not as I wish it to be or think it should be.

Something shifted for me that day. I realized that to pause is one of the most productive actions I can take.

In that pause, I not only felt better but also felt more clarity. Productivity is often associated with doing more, as efficiently as possible. What this commonplace definition of productivity fails to ask is if I am doing what is needed or useful? Or am I doing for the sake of doing? Which is ironically counter productive. It is better to not *do* than to expend resources (time, energy, money) *doing* what is not needed or not useful.

Determining what is useful or not is difficult, as my emotions can supersede my rational analysis. My emotional state can vary from feeling relaxed, calm, or happy, to feeling stressed, frustrated, or anxious. Within a single day or within a single hour.

When the feeling of being productive also leaves me also feeling tired, exhausted and spent, I naturally begin to find outlets to relax. And then end up in this yo-yo of going between feeling productive and feeling relaxed.

There are moments when I am engaged with what feel like "relaxing" activities, like sitting in meditation, swimming in the sea, cooking a meal, getting a massage, or hanging out with friends. There are other moments when I am engaged with what feel like "productive" activities, such as driving to get somewhere, clearing my inbox, monitoring the stock market, or working out with my trainer. This feeling of productivity is the culprit, as the feeling is often misguided and has side effects.

Before, if I wanted to feel more relaxed more often, my assumption was that I needed to make more time and space for "relaxing" activities, while reducing or eliminating the "productive" activities.

It was all very binary. I was essentially saying, "At this moment I am doing something 'relaxing,' so I am relaxed and not productive, and at this next moment, I am doing something 'productive,' so I cannot be relaxed."

I am not convinced that simply doing more "productive" activities is the solution to feeling more productive.

My experiment is to combine the two states of relaxation and productivity into a single state. And I have been doing this by bringing a "relaxed" quality to as many of the "productive" activities I engage in.

A relaxed quality involves a level of detachment from the outcome of the activity.

If I am working on a business deal, that means being detached from the specifics of the deal. If I am working out with my trainer, that means being detached from how many pushups or squats I do today. If I am investing in the stock market, that means being detached from the gains or losses.

It is counter-intuitive for sure. I have learned that trying to be productive all the time itself is not draining, but being attached to the outcomes of my productivity is massively draining. Things rarely go the way I desire them to, and the constant stress and anxiety associated with not getting what I want is heavy. It's not relaxing at all.

To *do* without expectation is to *be*. I'm reminded of punchline of the Bhagavad Gita, the ancient Hindu yogic philosophy. One has the right to the effort, but not the right to the fruit of their effort.

Productivity is a feeling in the end. And to cultivate that

feeling, on a sustained basis, I need to also feel relaxed along the way. Otherwise the feeling of productivity does not feel very good.

And that is how I unlearned busyness.

EXPERIMENT REFLECTIONS

Real productivity balances doing and being, learning finding joy and purpose in both states.

Learning to detach from specific outcomes while engaging in tasks makes the journey much more enjoyable.

Productivity is not about doing more things but about doing the right things, which means understanding what's actually important.

UNLEARNING
STRUGGLE

THREE YEARS OF
EFFORTLESS LIVING

Seeking means: having a goal. But finding
means: being free, being open, having no goal.
                                        -Osho

T he morning started off like none other.

I woke up naturally with a smile on my face. My bedroom in Lisbon is pitch black, thanks to blackout blinds, and without any clocks or natural light, I have no concept of time. This is intentional.

As my eyes opened, I softly said out loud to my voice assistant, "Hey Google, what time is it?" The voice responded, "10:36 a.m."

In what felt like a fraction of a fraction of a fraction of a second, I calmly observed to myself how I had already missed four meetings.

And then I became curious, still lying there in bed in my pitch-dark bedroom. Has this ever happened before? I wondered, and drew a blank. I could not think of a single example of when I had slept in this late.

I slowly got out of bed, went into my bright sun-filled living room with a sweeping view of Lisbon, and picked up my phone. Without even checking text messages, Whatsapp, email, or my missed calls, I said to my other voice assistant, "Hey Siri, call Ricardo."

The ringing stopped as Ricardo answered the call, not with a *Good morning* or *Hi, Kunal,* but with a shameless, "Are you alive?"

"Yes."

"You slept in," he said to me, with full confidence.

"Yes."

"Okay, don't worry, I've rearranged your schedule. How long until you can make it to the office?"

"I'll be there in twenty minutes."

"See you soon."

And just like that, I proceeded with my day. Without tension and anxiety.

It was only then that I realized what had happened. My body, having just returned to Lisbon from New York the day before, had adjusted to New York time.

Timing is everything. And often underappreciated. I have a long-standing pattern of being late to everything—at least to things at a micro level. But at a macro level, it's different. For the big stuff, I have learned a lot about how to be on time. When I am in flow with time, choices become easy. When I am attempting to force time, everything feels difficult.

Timing feels like an experiment. Without complete information, I am making a bet and leaning into it to see if it will work.

My journey as an entrepreneur and investor has been a clear example of experimenting with timing. I've had my fair share of trying to force outcomes—like squeezing out a product launch within an unrealistic deadline or trying to secure funding in an unfavorable economic climate. These were mostly uphill battles, like swimming against the current. And whenever I tried to force something, it never worked out well. I ended up drowning.

On the other hand, flowing is more akin to floating down the river of time. When I spontaneously moved to Portugal on three days' notice, I didn't force it. Instead, I allowed myself to be carried by the tide. When I reflect back on my journey here, it seemed as if the universe was conspiring to make it happen. I was on time.

At a lively group dinner one night in Lisbon, I met a charming couple who had been splitting their time between Puerto Rico and Lisbon. When I asked one of them how he ended up in Puerto Rico, he shared that after living in New York for a few years, he had moved permanently onto his boat there. During one of the tropical seasonal storms, he got shipwrecked in Puerto Rico.

Fast forward six years: he had set up a beautiful life, several local businesses, and a loving relationship. When I asked his partner where they met, she said Puerto Rico. But then she delivered the punchline: they were both from the same neighborhood in Los Angeles, had been at the same events and weddings, even briefly at the same high school, yet had never crossed paths. Until they did.

When I started my first tech company at twenty-one, I had absolutely no idea what I was doing. Neither did anyone else in the industry I was in. The technology at the time was difficult. *Very* difficult. Yet it did not feel like we were forcing anything, despite running into continuous issues. The business flowed, as we were on time.

To recognize when I am too early, on time, or too late on the big stuff requires me to sit in an observer state. I have to get out of the daily routine and grind, step back, and gain perspective. Perspective that is informed with a variety of information. I need to know what's going on around me and within me to assess timing and adjust the decision.

To make a big decision, be it professional or personal, often does require a leap of faith, and that is the hardest part. If I wait for all of the information to become clear, be it about a business opportunity, a romantic interest, a health routine, or a travel destination, I am probably too late.

As I have grown older and experienced first-hand being early, on time, and late, I've developed a different rhythm, a generally slower beat that often puts me on a different timeline than those around me. I can take a longer-term view more comfortably than most.

Living in Portugal over the past three years has taught me to surrender to the flow of time and embrace the unpredictability of each day. It has taught me that life isn't just about business meetings and ticking off items on a to-do list. It's also about spontaneous dinner dates, long walks along the beach, and savoring a three-hour lunch in the middle of the day. It's about how I feel in the present moment, irrespective of the ticking clock.

Although I often poke fun at the Southern European culture of being late to everything, there is a deeper wisdom here that I am slowly learning: **how to flow and not force.** The relative lack of reliability compared to the North American efficiency machine I have grown up with has helped me learn to relax and pay attention to what actually matters in life.

As a result, I am less agitated when the handyman doesn't show up, when the real estate viewing gets canceled after I've already arrived, or the restaurant closes early for a private event right as our main course is served.

I'm no longer the person I was when I lived in New York. Now, I choose to flow with the rhythm of my day, allowing myself to fully engage in each moment rather than constantly thinking about the next. It was a conscious experiment to learn how to flow, not force.

And that is how I unlearned struggle.

EXPERIMENT REFLECTIONS

Flow is achieved when I am fully present and engaged in the moment, without the internal distractions.

Balancing structure with spontaneity allows me to experience life's natural rhythm and not try to force things.

Letting go of control and embracing the unfolding process leads to a state of flow and a harmony with reality.

UNLEARNING MONEY

SIX SOURCES OF WEALTH

Effort does not lead to growth and it does not lead to change. At best it leads to repression and a covering of the root disease.

-Krishnamurti

My favorite cartoon as a kid was *DuckTales*. Not only were the voices of the main characters (Huey, Louie, and Dewey) funny but there was often a scene of Scrooge McDuck swimming in a swimming pool full of gold coins. I found it funny every time the brother ducks did something to upset the uncle. It usually involved him losing his coins.

Growing up, I associated being rich with having a lot of money. The word "currency" had one meaning: money. But over the years, I've found myself developing a far more personal—and more valuable—relationship with the concept of a currency.

What I am discovering is that, unlike the currency used to trade money, I have my own unique currency in life. Everyone does. This currency influences what I do far more than money does; it also influences what I avoid. Like any currency, it is meant to be exchanged.

My experiment with what it means to be rich has changed what I seek and desire to feel wealthy.

<u>My currency is inspiration.</u> Inspiration is what I love to receive, and try to give.

For example, when I moved to New York, I was drawn to the city, as it inspired me with the feeling that anything was possible. Wherever I live, I like to feel inspired by my space.

The people I feel the closest to also inspire me in their own ways. Some are inspirational by how they share themselves with me. Others encourage me to do what I dream to do. And others inspire me by simply being themselves, unconsciously modelling qualities and traits I wish to cultivate in myself.

When I think about the many items that have overstayed their welcome on my to-do list, the emails I haven't responded to in weeks, or the stretches I know are good for my tight shoulders that I still manage to avoid, I see clearly that none of these inspires me. They feel effortful; I do not have any currency to trade in them.

During a chat with a close friend, I shared my experiment to rethink what it meant to be rich, and we got talking about this idea of having a currency to trade in throughout life. As I shared more about my currency, he started to reflect on what his currency might be.

<u>My friend shared that his currency is connection.</u> He is most alive when he feels connected to the people in his presence, connected to the place he is living in, and connected to the work he is responsible for. It fuels him, feeds him, and fires him up.

My father's currency is curiosity. When we saw a documentary together about our changing planet, watching him watch the documentary was as interesting as watching the documentary itself for me. He loved every moment of it. He is constantly curious about other people's stories, always asking questions and exploring new ideas out loud.

My mother's currency is learning. She is always asking me questions about how to use different apps on her phone and better manage files and photos on her laptop. She browses the internet like a fiend, reading about random topics, often sharing with my sister and me what she discovers. Learning lights her up inside.

My brother-in-law's currency is creativity. Whether behind the camera, in front of the screen, with a paintbrush, or cooking in the kitchen, he is clearly happiest when he has the space and freedom to express his creativity. It's inspiring to see how creative he can be. It's impossible to guess what he is going to create next.

My sister's currency is fairness. She is at peace when there is justice, equity, and balance, be it for her or—more importantly—for others. She is also disheartened when there is a lack of fairness that she witnesses or experiences. Where my response is often intellectual, hers is visceral and all-consuming. Her passion grows when something is unfair.

There's a scene in the movie *The Iron Lady*, the story of British Prime Minister Margaret Thatcher, that has stuck with me. Thatcher, now in old age and retired from public life, walks into her doctor's office. The doctor innocently asks her, "How do you feel?" She turns to look out of the window, and begins her brief but powerful monologue.

Watch your thoughts for they become words.
Watch your words for they become actions.
Watch your actions for they become habits.
Watch your habits for they become your character.
And watch your character for it becomes your destiny.
What we think, we become. And I think I feel fine.

I love the reminder in this poetic monologue to pay attention to what I pay attention to.

This is why mindfulness practices have spoken to me for so long, not only as a tool to calm down and relax but also as a tool to become more aware of my thinking. My thinking becomes my life and my experience of it.

My currency in life is my North Star, and my attention is the rocket ship to get me there. Together they act as a compass to help navigate the big and small decisions. Together, they help me understand why I am drawn to certain places, people, and ideas—and why I avoid others.

When my attention is focused on what I do not have and what I feel is missing in my life, I begin to feel impoverished. The opportunities for comparison, be it through digital and social media, stories in the news, or even when I compare my fantasy to my reality, are the situations where I start to feel poor.

When my attention is focused on what I do have and am grateful for, I begin to feel rich. I appreciate the people in my life and those not in my life; the opportunities I have received and also the ones I have not; the challenges I have overcome, and the ones I have yet to overcome. When my attention is fixed on what I appreciate in my reality, I feel rich.

Money is a form of stored energy, in a way. **When I am trading in my true currency, it is a way of *gathering* energy.** Trading in my currency of inspiration eventually allowed me to make enough money. Being in the fortunate situation of having enough money, one of the highest uses of it for me is to further invest it back into my currency of inspiration.

When I am trading in my currency and paying attention to the right things, I am most alive, most myself, and most in alignment with my natural state and energy. I feel rich, regardless of how much money I do or don't have at that moment.

And that is how I unlearned money.

EXPERIMENT REFLECTIONS

When my attention is focused on what I do have and am grateful for, I begin to feel rich. I appreciate the people in my life and the opportunities I have received, which brings a sense of wealth and fulfilment.

Trading in my currency creates a cycle of energy that transcends monetary wealth.

Feeling rich is about being most alive and aligned with my natural state and energy, regardless of how much money I have at the moment

UNLEARNING
LONELINESS

ONE SURPRISE ACT OF KINDNESS

> *The greatest disease in the world today is being unwanted, unloved, and uncared for. We can cure physical diseases with medicine, but the only cure for loneliness, despair, and hopelessness is love. There are many in the world who are dying for a piece of bread but there are many more dying for a little love.*
>
> -Anthony De Mello

I n London on a Friday evening, I made a choice on a whim: to have dinner alone at a busy restaurant—without my phone in hand. As I sat down, taking in my surroundings, the bustling energy of the place inspired me. I was content to be alone and observe the people around me. But then the couple sitting next to me struck up a conversation.

We were soon sharing food and laughter. I was touched by how kind, fun, and grounded they were. They made me feel like a part of their world, and I felt grateful for their warmth. My aloneness allowed me to notice things and appreciate people in new ways. It was a reminder of the beauty and connection that can be found in unexpected places.

I finished my meal before they did and got up to pay. An experiment was brewing in my mind.

When speaking with the waitress, I asked her to charge me for the table next to me and not tell them until after I'd left. She was surprised. She assumed I wanted to pay for the table on the other side of me, where four young women were having dinner. But I said no. The couple. The waitress was touched by the action. We even added dessert, with a candle on top. I don't know what they were celebrating, but assumed they'd find something to celebrate.

As I walked out of the restaurant, a wave of energy flowed

through me. Then I started to tear up. These people had opened their evening to me, sharing their dinner, their conversation, their true selves. Though I wouldn't get to enjoy their reaction to my experiment, it was pretty easy for me to imagine it.

By being kind to me—the stranger at the next table—this couple had shown me love. And that love inspired me to be kind to them, in my own unique way. The impact of unexpected kindness can be difficult to describe, so it is best experienced. It can be felt on an energetic and spiritual level. It's a deep sense of alignment with the universe: a recognition that **we are all connected and part of something greater than ourselves.**

To be kind is to love. And when I act from a place of love, I tap into that connection and feel a sense of purpose, along with the joy that often accompanies it. That evening, the feeling of kindness was a physical sensation. It started as a warmth in my chest, spreading throughout my body, then radiated outward. It was like a flow of electrical energy that connected me to the people and world around me through openness and vulnerability.

In that moment, all my problems disappeared. And that is the power of love.

Love is transformative. It has the power to shift the energy in a room, transform a stranger into a friend, and create a ripple effect that extends far beyond the immediate moment. When I am loving toward others, I am planting seeds of goodness that have the power to grow and spread throughout the world.

Love is not just about doing something nice for someone else. It is also an act of self-care and self-kindness. When I am loving to others, I am also loving to myself. It allows me to tap into a deeper sense of compassion and empathy, reminding me everyone needs connection.

The impact of unconditional love can be profound. It shows humanity's capacity for goodness. Unconditional love allows me to see the world through a different lens, one that is open and expansive, filled with possibility.

It's easy to get caught up in the hustle and bustle of daily life, to disconnect from myself and those around me. Simple acts of unconditional love remind me that I am not here alone on Hotel Earth. **In a world that can often feel overwhelming and isolating, acts of unexpected kindness offer a glimmer of hope.**

If I learned kindness from anyone, it was my parents. They were the first to show me that kindness and unconditional love can go hand in hand.

It was not until my parents became grandparents, though, that my understanding of the unconditional love that a parent gives a child became clearer to me.

My sister and brother-in-law graciously took the monkey off my back by having a baby, fulfilling my parents' desire to be grandparents. Kavi, my nephew, is one of my favorite people in the world, evident by the joy I feel every time I look at my phone and see his face on my wallpaper.

My parents transformed into different people once Kavi checked into Hotel Earth. My sister and I remark to each other often how much our parents appeared to have changed. We hear sounds from our parents' mouths we never knew existed. We see genuine joy and laughter, again somewhat unfamiliar to our eyes. Who are these people who are supposedly our parents?

The love I see my parents give their grandson is so noticeable, it even sparked a hint of envy within me—until I realized that I, too, receive the same unconditional love from them. The love and affection I feel toward my nephew, and that I observe my parents give him, is the same type of love I have received my entire life from my parents, family and friends.

It touches my heart to now know I am loved in this way. That I have been, that I am today, and that I will be in the future. Unconditionally. It is no longer an intellectual belief, but an emotional, embodied experience.

No experiment necessary here. The result is known.

As an introspective and reflective person, I have given my parents a harder time than they deserve in my journal, my blog posts, my books and in sharing with my therapist and friends. In the past I have often associated the less likable aspects of who or how I am with my parents. It is easier for me to place blame externally than to take ownership internally.

My parents are my parents. I used to think they had to change to be less annoying to me. And they *are* changing—but not how I expected. They are changing, in their own ways, in their own time and at their own pace.

Having connected with the unconditional love my parents have for me, and the kindness they show me no matter what I do or don't do, is remarkable. It has enabled me to show that same loving kindness toward myself, and to others. I understand them better now that I have seen their love through the eyes of my nephew, who receives love from every direction, without really understanding or even acknowledging it.

When my parents say or do things I find annoying, I remember that their underlying intention is one of love. It doesn't always feel like love. But I have learned to tune into the depth of our relationship beyond our interactions on the surface. Time and again, my parents are kind to me, even when my own kindness slips.

Ram Dass's famous quote goes: "If you think you are enlightened, go live with your family for a week." When my parents first came to visit me in Portugal and stayed with me for several weeks, it gave us all of us plenty of time to test that hypothesis. It was an experiment and the outcome was encouraging. Staying with my parents turned out to be far more pleasant than I expected. The annoyance I'd sometimes felt in the past was gone—not because they had changed, but because *I* had changed. I was more connected to the unconditional love flowing in both directions.

And that is how I unlearned loneliness.

EXPERIMENT REFLECTIONS

Unconditional love is a powerful force that shapes our ability to love ourselves and others.

What I observed in my parents when they became grandparents helped me realize that I, too, am loved unconditionally.

Experiencing unconditional love changes our perspective, making us more compassionate and empathetic towards others.

UNLEARNING DEATH

SEVEN DEATHS THAT SHAPED ME

We do not 'come into' this world; we come out of it, as leaves from a tree.

-Alan Watts

W hen I lived in New York, my parents came for a visit that will forever be remembered. We went out for fancy meals at fun restaurants around the city, and they completely took over my apartment, fixing all the things I didn't even know needed fixing. We had a great time. Until the energy took a drastic turn.

We learned that my uncle, who lived just outside the city in Staten Island, had just been moved to hospice care. He was eighty-five years old and had lived a life rich in meaning and purpose. A real pioneer in the family, he moved from India to the United States in his thirties with absolutely nothing. Building the kind of life fairy tales are made of, his generosity and kindness had been felt not only by our family but by the entire community.

We went to see him. I felt nervous on the ride over. I knew it would be the closest I'd ever been to death as an adult. The last time someone passed away in our family, I was a young teenager.

My uncle was resting in a small room on the lower level of the building. It was quiet and peaceful, without much inside it—only a bed, a few chairs, a couch, a small flower vase. The sliding door to the backyard was open. We heard the birds chirping and felt the cool air blowing through the screen door. Fall sun drenched us in soft light. It felt like a waiting room between this world and the next.

And as I sat there with my dying uncle, it inspired a short poem. I wrote it on a piece of paper and taped it to the wall beside him.

With your boarding pass in hand
You made it through security
And are now waiting at the gate
This is your final flight
It will be time to board soon
We will miss you
Bon voyage.

This flight my uncle was about to take did not have first class, business, or economy. He would take it without any material belongings. I found that a humbling thought about what is truly important in life, remembering my experiment to not buy stuff.

Although I've meditated, journaled, read about, and discussed the topic of death many times, that day was different. Feeling, touching, and hearing death up close, both through my uncle and my relatives, took a theoretical concept and made it real. Seeing my parents—spring chickens compared to my uncle—express their emotions deepened my understanding of mortality.

I noticed a shift inside me that afternoon. An urgency about life was born that day that has stayed with me. The same night we said goodbye to my uncle, I signed up to do a yoga teacher training course. It was a big commitment: 200 hours spread out over the next nine months. I'd decided long ago that I would do the training at some point, always thinking "later." But later was conditional: conditional on me making more time and conditional on feeling more confident in my own yoga practice first.

I have a timeline in life. Everyone does. That day, I committed to do what's important to me, to reach for what my heart desires before my final flight departs.

That day was a reminder that life does not wait. If something is important, that alone is enough reason to make it an unconditional priority. Do it now, not later.

I realized that a fear of death that trails me like a shadow is not actually what it seems. The fear of death is, in fact, a fear of living. This insight has begun to reshape my understanding of how to live.

My daily life is filled with meticulous care and calculated decisions. I'm careful while crossing the street, vigilant behind the steering wheel of my car. I find myself assessing the risks, like a background computer processor is always evaluating potential investments, unconsciously forecasting potential gains and probability of losses.

At times I can hesitate before opening myself to friends or potential romantic partners, building walls to protect my vulnerability. I obsess over what I eat, ensuring I'm fueling my body with the right nutrients. I watch my words, aiming to strike the perfect balance of honesty and political correctness. These actions are united by a common thread: the fear of death. But it's not merely the dread of physical demise, like my uncle experienced. It's the fear of reputational death, the death of relationships, the death of emotions, and the death of ego. Each careful step, every cautious word, is an attempt to avoid these metaphorical deaths.

Yet, the more I reflect, the more an underlying paradox emerges: **In trying to avoid death, I am, in a way, avoiding life itself.** Every day, I am bound by an invisible chain, shackled by the fear of death, resulting in a life cautiously lived. A life constrained.

When I delve into thoughts about death, I feel a profound sense of urgency bubbling within me, reminding me of the temporary nature of my existence here on Hotel Earth. It's a stark realization of the fragility of my life, a poignant reminder of its impermanence.

However, acknowledging the inevitability of death does

not imply embracing it prematurely. Far from it. While I would never consciously accelerate death, I now understand that I can, and should, choose to embrace living more fully.

Life is not meant to be merely a series of safe choices and guarded interactions. It's meant to be lived fully and fearlessly, embracing all the risks and rewards. This is the grand experiment of life itself.

I strive to live more freely, unburdened by the fear of the metaphorical deaths that have held me back. I aim to breathe deeply, taste new experiences, and explore unfamiliar territories. I'm learning to express myself more candidly, to be more honest in my interactions and be more vulnerable, opening myself to deep and meaningful connections.

In my quest for good health, I'm evolving to understand that wellbeing extends beyond physicality. It's about nourishing the mind, the soul, as well as the body. It's about embracing life in its entirety, from the rush of adrenaline to the tranquility of meditation, and from the joy of accomplishment to the sting of failure.

The experiments I have shared in this book have all involved me bringing death to seven ideas.

Death to the assumption I had about how to live.

Death to the assumption that buying stuff would bring me happiness.

Death to the expectation that home was based on my physical space.

Death to desire to always be in control and know everything in advance.

Death to a fear of heights.

Death to my North American lifestyle and mindset.

Death to my identity being linked to my business.

To live involves a lot of death. I'm learning to let go of my fear of death and embrace it as a part of life. It's a major perspective shift to see that death is not the antithesis of life but an ingredient. It's not a full stop but a poignant pause: a serene sunset at the end of a vibrant day.

And that is how I unlearned death.

EXPERIMENT REFLECTIONS

Learning to die involves letting go of fear and embracing it. Seeing everything I experience as an integral part of my journey.

Inviting death to my old beliefs and assumptions that no longer serve me is how I learn to live.

Death enables me to live more fully, appreciating each moment and the connections I have with others.

UNLEARNING HAPPINESS

TWO CHOICES THAT CHANGE EVERYTHING

The world is not imperfect or slowly evolving along a path to perfection. No, it is perfect at every moment.

-Alan Watts

Over the course of my lifetime thus far, I've had the privilege of meeting many highly accomplished people who inspired me. But one in particular has been the most inspiring person I have ever met for a range of reasons.

He walks through the world without any fear. He climbs mountains for the sheer joy of the challenge, focused on the journey, not the destination. For him, life is not a series of transactions; it is a series of experiences.

He is unconcerned with how he looks. If he has bedhead, bad breath, stains on his clothes, or holes in his pants, none of it matters to him.

He does not care what others think about him. If he is in a crowded public space or in his quiet bedroom, he speaks with the same tone and uses the same vocabulary.

He truly loves everyone he comes across, unconditionally. He will smile at strangers without hesitation, although he can be a little shy at first when seeing someone new. He will quietly examine the person to see if it's safe for him to engage—and then engage without holding anything back.

He knows how to express his needs and wants clearly and does not stop until he feels that he's been heard. In this way, he is at peace and does not store any resentment.

He is infinitely curious about the world. In each new space he enters, he likes to inspect every corner, every button, every object, every person.

He is always open to hearing what you have to say and will always tell you what he thinks. There is no guessing where you stand; he will make it clear.

He is completely present and absorbed in the moment, never dwelling on the past, and he seems totally uninterested in planning the future.

The most inspiring person I have ever met is my young nephew, Kavi. In his relatively short time here on Hotel Earth, he has taught me so much about how to be happy. Specifically, how to be present and curious about everything and everyone.

I aspire to be more like him when I grow up. He is happy with life.

My journey to discover happiness started a decade ago, when I reached the top of a mountain I had been climbing and found only dissatisfaction and disappointment waiting for me. I had a burning desire to rediscover what I believed to be true—and I put myself intentionally through a lot of discomfort to find out.

From my early experiments to not buy stuff and go houseless by sleeping on stranger's couches, to committing to meditation on a long-term basis, to discovering how to disconnect from devices, and ultimately learning how to conquer long-held fears, I built a confidence and resilience that I will be okay, regardless of what happens. The Bali adventure put this confidence to the test. And I passed.

Feeling energized by how I was growing in all of this discomfort, I spontaneously moved to Portugal, curious to see how I would do. Not only did I do well: I made a lot of new friends I very much appreciate to this day. To make the space for new places and people, I had to learn how to disassociate with my business as the only slice of my professional identity.

Having learned that being on time is itself an experiment, one that involves taking risks and a leap of faith, I now have the confidence to keep doing it, again and again. Redefining what it means to be rich has given me an unlimited source of fuel for my journey, while continuing to stay grounded in the unconditional love and kindness that my parents and family have given me over the years.

I have been reminded more than I'd like that everyone is here on Hotel Earth for a temporary stay, and that living involves dying.

The biggest belief that has died in my mind over this journey is the idea that life is conditional. I have long held the belief that *once this, then that*. Be it in business, romance, health, community, politics, money, weather, culture, or friends. I have wasted countless moments of my life in the false belief that once I get what I want, then I will be happy.

Ten years ago, I had everything I wanted—and I was not happy. I then had no choice but to question this belief; to remove the conditionality on life, one part at a time.

My biggest lesson through a decade of experimentation is that **life is not conditional**. It is not conditional on where I live, how much money I have, how many friends I have, how healthy I am, how well liked I am, or anything of the like.

The moment I remove the conditionality I place on life, I begin to notice it is in my nature to be happy. I realize that I have always been happy, I just didn't know it. I was conditioned to believe otherwise, and through a lot of effort and discomfort, I unconditioned myself to return back to my original factory settings, similar to my three-year-old nephew.

In the face of any discomfort or disappointment, I see now I have two choices:

Choice one: rearrange the world to my liking.

The choice I make when I try to arrange things, people, society, and situations in a way that I believe they ought to be, according to my beliefs. This is good and that is bad. This is right and that is wrong.

I made this choice for most of my life. Trying to control the outside world was exhausting, and if it appeared to work, I was only fooling myself. I had little control over what happened and naively made my happiness conditional on what happened.

Choice two: realign my thinking to reality.

The choice I make when I recognize that I get to choose how to respond to reality. This choice is like carrying an umbrella in the rain. When it was raining, I could complain about it—or I could pull out my umbrella and carry on without any concern, anxiety, frustration, worry, or stress.

The umbrella is my attitude.

There will of course be unwanted and unpleasant moments along my journey. Instead of obsessing about minimizing or eliminating them, I can focus instead on being prepared for them, with the confidence that I can deal with whatever will come my way. Over time, I stop labeling these moments as unwanted or unpleasant. I see them simply as part of reality.

The second choice is how I have learned to create a life with less friction and more ease. A life that aspires to be in flow and harmony with reality, where everlasting, boundless, unconditional happiness exists.

This happiness bears little resemblance to the kind of happiness I thought would be waiting at the top of the mountain all those years ago, as I stared at my identical Reiss shirts and realized something was missing. I had to cast off my pack, the heavy burden of values and beliefs I'd inherited yet never thought to question.

Every experiment brought me closer to understanding myself.

Every lesson opened my mind.

Every emotion—tears, laughter, loneliness, love—opened my heart.

And when I began that journey, everything changed forever.

I had finally unlearned how to live.

EXPERIMENT REFLECTIONS

The belief that happiness is conditional on external circumstances in my life took me further away from the feelings of happiness.

My journey to rediscover happiness involved unlearning through experimentation, and learning how to discover my own beliefs and values.

Choosing to align my thinking with my reality, rather than trying to control the world around me, has led to a life with less friction and more ease.

Thank you for taking the time to read *UNLEARNING*.

Online reviews are incredibly important for authors and readers alike. They help new readers discover books they'll love and encourage authors like me to continue writing.

If you enjoyed *UNLEARNING*, please leave a review on Amazon. Scan the QR code below on your phone to easily and quickly leave a review.

Scan me

ACKNOWLEDGMENTS

My ability to experiment is directly related to how my parents supported, raised and encouraged me to always go for it. My sister has been my cheerleader, always there to give me her unsolicited advice and my brother-in-law is a source of creative inspiration. *Thank you mom, dad, Kanika and Amit for shaping my life.*

My close friends, past girlfriends, and colleagues teach me so much about myself, from the awkward moments to the moments of brilliance. *Thank you all for choosing to be in my life, and for continuing to tolerate me.*

And to you, the reader, thank you for your interest in my journey and I hope it has inspired you to experiment with discovering how you want to live.

About the Author

Kunal Gupta is an entrepreneur, investor, and author known for his insightful and unique perspectives grounded in his life experiences.

UNLEARNING is Kunal's first book, based on a series of experiments he conducted voluntarily looking for growth and meaning. His other writing includes what he has learned about business, technology, mindfulness, and health, reflecting his passions and expertise.

Born, raised, and educated in Canada, Kunal studied software engineering from the University of Waterloo and artificial intelligence at the University of Oxford.

Kunal founded and successfully scaled an advertising technology company, serving as Chief Everything Officer for 15 years. Based in New York at the time, he had the opportunity to see the world, collaborating with teams and clients across 30+ countries.

Deeply committed to mindfulness and mental health, he integrates these principles into his everyday life and enjoys sharing them with those around him regularly.

Engage with Kunal live at **kunalgpt.com**
Follow his blog and newsletter at **howto.live**
Discover more about his journey at **kunalgupta.live**

Kunal is donating 100% of book proceeds to mental health charities.

Made in the USA
Las Vegas, NV
22 September 2024